P9-DXT-569

PRAISE FOR

SILENCING THE ENEMY WITHIN

"Marsha Rene delivers a powerful reminder that addiction is an actual disease, one that takes root in its victims' profound pains—not in their lack of willpower. Her chronicling of her journey from death-defying abysses to the triumphant light of recovery doubles as a gift of love and a tremendous education."

—J-L Deher-Lesaint, Assistant Professor of English, City Colleges of Chicago

"Marsha Rene dives into the roots of her risky, self-destructive behavior and vividly takes readers along on her journey to recovery. After a decade of hardcore substance abuse, she emerges as a healer with numerous valuable lessons to impart. Her brutal honesty about the toll of addiction and the difficulty of releasing oneself from its grip makes her the perfect messenger."

—Tori Marlan, Award-Winning Immersive Journalist, USA and Canada

"As someone who has battled addiction myself, Marsha Rene's story of self-exploration and eventual victory over her demons resonated with me. This is a wonderful story that can help many. Refreshing!"

—Cleo Baker, Former Lead Book Club Moderator, Chicago Public Library

Silencing the Enemy Within:
A Memoir of Addiction and Healing

by Marsha Rene with Cheryl Ross

ISBN 978-1-64663-205-3

Published by

3705 Shore Drive
Virginia Beach, VA 23455
800-435-4811
www.koehlerbooks.com

SILENCING THE ENEMY WITHIN

A MEMOIR OF ADDICTION AND HEALING

MARSHA RENE

WITH CHERYL ROSS

VIRGINIA BEACH
CAPE CHARLES

This book is dedicated to Paul B. and all others who have died because of addiction. You are gone but never forgotten.

AUTHOR'S NOTE

All the names of people in this book have been changed with the exception of my own, Paul B.'s, and Brett's. I have related all events that occurred when I was in active addiction to the best of my recollection.

TABLE OF CONTENTS

INTRODUCTION

Sweat prickled my skin as my anxiety kicked into high gear one winter day in 2003 at John F. Kennedy International Airport—two years after 9/11. A few days before, my mom had sprung a surprise trip to Denver, Colorado, on me to visit my brothers. The thought of flying more than halfway across the country put me on edge. The notion of flying itself didn't scare me; it was the length of time we'd be in the air. I had tried everything to get out of this trip, but my mom had already bought our tickets. Now, surrounded by airport security, with only my loving, poor mother and my mini-dachshund, Heidi, for support, I was living the nightmare of a lifetime.

For this long plane ride, I'd *had* to come prepared. Right under the elastic at the top of my panties, just below my belly button, sat a dozen postage-stamp-sized wax-paper baggies of heroin enveloped in one slim piece of paper. This was just enough heroin to keep me from getting dope sick—suffering from diarrhea, vomiting, the chills, and anxiety—while on the trip. The potential of falling ill for lack of drugs was what had made me so anxious about the hours on end of travel. Now, as security agents subjected me to post-9/11 checks—I don't remember them all precisely—I felt like I was on the verge of throwing up or passing out for fear of being caught! The seconds that passed felt like twelve million years. But next thing I knew, the agents let me continue through the line. Relief washed over me. I picked up my carry-on bag and Heidi and continued on my way to boarding.

I'm not proud of passing airport inspection post-9/11, but that day, I was grateful I did. After my mom and I boarded the plane and stored our luggage in the overhead bins and Heidi in her carrier under a seat, I found my way to the restroom. I locked myself in it, took down my pants, and fished out some heroin from my underwear. I snorted the illicit opioid to calm down.

How I handled this situation was typical of me at the time. For years, I had routinely lived on the edge, making reckless, self-destructive decisions like this over and over. I couldn't stop living this way because drugs ruled me. Throughout my teenage years and up to my mid-twenties, I allowed them to keep me stuck in a negative way of living. I could not pull myself out of this rut because my thinking, like my behavior, was diseased.

If you suffer from an addiction, you know what I'm talking about. I'm speaking of a way of thinking that makes you loathe yourself and constantly reach for a harmful outside source to solve an internal problem. It could be drugs, shopping, gambling, sex, love, alcohol, social media, vaping, you name it.

Fortunately, in my mid-twenties, I stopped using drugs. As I write this book, that was nearly seventeen years ago. Therapy, twelve-step work, prayer, meditation, and humbling myself before a higher power helped me leave that life behind and achieve personal and professional success. Today, I am a proud dog mommy, a public speaker, a mentor to drug addicts, and the owner of a successful holistic healing center that takes care of bodies, minds, and souls. I have blossomed into a loving, nurturing Reiki Master who administers healing massages to addicts, military veterans, pre-op and post-op patients, car accident victims, and the list goes on.

I live with integrity and am excited about what each new day will bring. This surprises me more than anything else because I used to think that I was going to die a junkie.

At one point, it seemed like I was on every illegal drug in existence. In addition to heroin, I did coke, crack, and ecstasy, just to name a few. My drug use had no boundaries. I couldn't stop using, so I couldn't keep jobs. I stole money to pay for drugs, lied for drugs, considered prostitution to pay for my habit, and dated men who kept me in the grip of addiction. When I tell you that I could not stop using drugs for anything, I mean it. I really could not stop.

My diseased thinking was in full effect. It left me feeling that I was not worth anything. I had to hit a very deep low, which included brushes with the law, getting fired, and putting myself at risk of dying, to see myself as someone who deserved better. Then I had to be open to help from others. For me, that meant religious attendance of twelve-step meetings and getting honest about my drug use and how it was harming me and other people. Once I reached that point, I was on my way to recovery and, ultimately, to becoming a better person. This is not a small statement because many people don't get out of drug addiction alive.

In the United States, from 1999 to present, drug overdoses appear to be on track to kill nearly a million people. Preliminary data from the Centers for Disease Control and Prevention shows that they may have taken the lives of some 72,000 Americans, a record, in 2019 alone. Experts predict that number may climb even higher in 2020 amidst the COVID-19 crisis for various reasons, including closures of, or cutbacks at, in-person supportive group gatherings and drug treatment and recovery centers. The US is a worldwide leader in drug overdose deaths, if not *the* leader, with an epidemic that has been reported to be largely fueled by illicit opioids as well as illicit stimulants.

This scourge has ravaged my friends of various racial and socioeconomic backgrounds. Many of them have died from overdosing on opioids and other drugs. When I consider that fact, I am extremely grateful for the bottom I hit at a young age and the people who encouraged me to rise above my addiction.

That's, in part, what this book, *Silencing the Enemy Within: A Memoir of Addiction and Healing,* is about: my struggle and success in recovery. But, to help you better understand some of the universal aspects of this disease that has killed so many people, it also provides a broader view of addiction. It looks at *why* I am an addict and what the disease of addiction really is. To that end, it traces the childhood and family forces that put me, in my case a white Jewish woman from a middle-class home, on the path to drug addiction; and it shows how the place I lived nearby and the decade I grew up in, drug-infested New York City in the 1990s, set the stage to allow my addiction to flourish. On the positive side, it also explores how the massage therapy career I was once fired from played a key role in my recovery.

Silencing the Enemy Within does not end with my triumph over active drug addiction. If it did, I would be telling you only a portion of my story and not providing you as much help as I could.

So, it also highlights a story that Hollywood doesn't always show you: that many addicts in recovery struggle with another addiction after they have put their biggest issue to bed. A lot of people think we get clean and *poof* our addictive behavior goes away. Not true, because the disease of addiction never goes away. Only two types of addicts exist: active and recovering. There are no "recovered" addicts.

Simply put, addiction cannot be cured because it is a mental illness. Some people may insist that it is a choice, not a disease; but it is an obsessive-compulsive urge to keep using, and I call that a mental illness—an insidious one. In one person, it can manifest itself in the form of more than one addiction. That's where the second part of my story picks up.

For years, I have struggled with another issue. It is rooted in the death of my father, who died relatively young, and in something ugly that happened to me as a teen. From there, it bloomed and expressed itself in my romantic life. My problem: For decades, I slept indiscriminately with many people and stayed involved with the wrong types of partners. After I stopped using drugs, these relationships spiraled out of control. As it was with drugs, the same went for partners. I had many and didn't always use protection. This showed me that, like other friends who struggled with more than one addiction, a hole in my soul still begged to be filled.

That's because the mind of an addicted person can be his or her worst enemy. Even when we're clean, a mean inner voice preys on us. It lies to us, and we believe the lies. It tells us that we aren't good enough or worthy of love or success, that we may as well just use or suffer or die because we are worthless.

Somewhere deep in my soul, I still felt unworthy of love and being treated well. It was that voice, my inner enemy as a result of my life history, telling me a lie. To this day, despite all of my business success, despite my nearly seventeen years clean, I have to constantly hush this voice to stay healthy and whole.

In *Silencing the Enemy Within*, you will see how I trace this voice back to the death of my father and the lack of a strong disciplinary presence in my house after he passed. I can also see how his own addiction—in his case, to cigarettes—signaled that I might have the addiction gene. Whether I was born with it, I went on to model many of my father's addictive behaviors . . . and, in my relationships with men, I took a cue from my mother, who struggled to sustain a strong romantic relationship after my father's death.

As I examine the roots of my addiction in this book, you can use my story for questions about the causes of your own addiction. For instance, what's the source of your inner voice? Whether your addiction is food, gambling, social media, sex, drugs, or some other substance or behavior, ponder other parallels in your story and use my story as an inspiration to understand your own inner enemy and overcome your active addiction.

If you're in recovery or an active addict, my story will show you that you don't need to be perfect to get or stay clean. You will see that, instead, people like us need to take extra special care of ourselves and never take our eyes off the ball of recovery. Time doesn't exempt us from relapse or hurting ourselves or acting out. That's why people who have been clean for decades still attend twelve-step meetings, the gatherings intended to help us stay off drugs, stay off alcohol, and stay away from other menacing substances or behaviors. Just remember that you have the power to stay on the right course and that you can live the life you want. I am an example of that, and many others are too.

If you're reading this and are not an addict but know someone who is, I hope my story will help you better understand addiction and what we go through. Hopefully, it will give you more respect for us and an understanding that we are doing the best that we can, that we are in recovery to get better, and that we are better—not perfect—people because of it. Be in our corner. Encourage us to continue to attend twelve-step meetings and to stay clean. Cheer us on.

So now, come with me on my journey of recovery. I'm about to share with you a story of identity, hope, faith, struggle, love, loss, mistakes, humanity, broken hearts, bad decisions, bad relationships, great relationships, business success, family, and the ups and downs of life in and out of recovery. It's a story about a woman that I don't know anymore. I no longer resemble her in the least, and if I can say that, you can say that about yourself too.

You don't have to keep living this way and don't have to die this way. Your life is worth fighting for, trust me.

PART ONE

THE DESCENT

CHAPTER ONE

A CHILDHOOD DIES

Hey, I didn't formally introduce myself, so allow me to do that now: I go by Marsha Rene, my first and middle names. After various rehabs, detoxes, and so many empty promises, and so many I'm sorries, I'll never do it agains, I didn't mean to do its, I never meant to hurt yous, I finally got clean on February 2, 2004.

At the end of my active drug addiction, I had nothing. I didn't have my health or my family's respect; they loved me, but they didn't like me very much. I was spiritually dead, lost, emptier than I'd ever felt. I was scared to live and scared to die. I was broken inside.

I hit many bottoms. Eventually, a twelve-step program lifted me up. The twelve steps are guiding principles that help people change their behavior to put their active addiction in the past. My sponsor, a person in the program with whom I shared my deepest feelings and fears, did not give up on me. Many others in the program were in my corner as well. All of this mental support helped me move forward. The program changed my life. It saved me. Before it, I was that desperate junkie on the street whom you looked upon with pity.

I had allowed drugs to take everything away from me—my self-respect and honor. I didn't care about myself or anyone else. My disease and self-centered thinking did not allow me to see outside myself. I knew what I was doing was wrong and I felt bad about it, but I could not break free from the storm. I was a tornado upending everyone's life that I touched, especially the lives of those who loved and cared for me. A vicious cycle of self-destruction devoured me.

The storm of addiction began to settle in when I was eight years old, the year my father died. His passing changed my family's world and put me on a downward spiral.

It marked the beginning of the end of my childhood.

Picture this: a nice three-story, four-bedroom colonial home in a racially mixed middle-class neighborhood in Suffolk County, in the suburbs of Long Island, New York. A father in a white-collar job, the breadwinner of the family. A largely stay-at-home mom with a part-time nursing job. A household of three children, two boys and a girl. Trips to a house of worship, in this case a temple, on major holidays, and to religious school. Prayers at the dinner table and frequent visits with extended family.

For many years growing up, that was my world.

To understand my descent into addiction, you have to understand my background. Many people say that who we become starts at home, and I think that idea applies to me. In my case, the key to understanding why I started down the fast path to addiction rests with my dad. When he died, my family's link to a world that he had largely created snapped and we lost our sense of identity. This profoundly impacted my ability to cope and led me to escape into drugs.

The family identity we inherited from Dad had come to life thousands of miles away, before Dad was even a thought. It was born in the Holocaust and fully grew—and exploded—after Dad married and started a family.

The twentieth-century genocide that took the lives of millions of Jewish people is a topic that my surviving family members of that horrific time in history don't like to say much about, so what I'm about to tell you is pretty much the extent of what I know. Dad's parents and his two sisters survived the Holocaust. Somehow, the four of them escaped death in a Romanian concentration camp. In the fall of 1946, in their home in Romania, Dad was born, and about three years later, the family moved to Israel.

The survival of Dad's immediate family members was not the norm for dozens of other members of his extended family, many of whom died in the Holocaust. Dad must have had it rough growing up because his parents and sisters suffered from post-traumatic stress disorder, which must have vicariously affected Dad. As he became a young man, I'm sure he balanced finding his own identity as someone who did not endure the Holocaust with the tension from his family members who did experience it.

In the late 1950s, Dad's family immigrated to the United States from Israel seeking a better life. They settled in Washington Heights, a New York City neighborhood that many European Jews had fled to in the previous two decades to escape Nazism. Dad arrived knowing his native Yiddish and not very much English, which he would learn from a friend. Meanwhile, his mother and father kept the household running, both working as tailors in a New York City garment factory.

My *zayde* and *bubbe* (Yiddish for "grandfather" and "grandmother," respectively) ran a superstrict household, raising their children to get an education, marry, and achieve professional success. No way would Dad and his sisters do anything but well in life.

Dad was good with his hands, artistically inclined, and a good student at the High School of Art and Design, a vocational school that taught him how to apply his artistic gifts in a profession. After high school, he served in the Army and later attended a community college in New York City, where he studied structural steel detailing. In his career, he would create the blueprints for the interior steel structures of buildings and be involved in impressive projects such as museums, shopping centers, and the Nassau Coliseum, a big arena on Long Island that I would enjoy many a rock show at as an adult.

But even before his career took off, Dad, six feet tall, balding, olive-skinned with light-brown eyes, mustachioed, and typically dressed in smart, classic American blue jeans and polo shirts, was already a pretty good catch. On a blind date in his twenties, he met the twentysomething woman who would become the focus of his affections. This striking five-foot-six beauty, a nurse with wavy light-brown hair, captivated him with her piercing blue eyes. Like him, she was Jewish, but her immediate family, whose roots were in Russia, Poland, and Austria, had lived in the United States for many years and did not share the same Holocaust legacy as Dad's family. About six months after meeting, this woman from the North Bronx and Dad set their sights on getting married.

Their marriage first resulted in two boys, several years apart, and finally, when Mom was twenty-nine and Dad was in his early thirties, a girl, me!

I write that with an exclamation point because I'm told that my birth made Dad overflow with happiness. He had been praying for a girl, and when I arrived in the summer of 1979, snagging my place as a member of Generation X—the generation that would grow up in the midst of a raging crack epidemic and on grunge music, hip hop, and alternative rock—he literally ran up and down the hospital hall from joy.

I was the apple of Dad's eye, literally and figuratively. I got his light-brown eyes, and like him, I would one day need glasses. I also got a little mole on top of my left eyebrow, just like he had. Relatives would kid us and say that I was my dad from "the nose up." Thankfully, however, that excluded my hair. Unlike him, I had a lot of it, and it was light brown and wavy like my mother's.

As a baby and toddler, my parents showed me so much love. They sang lullabies together to help me fall asleep. One song went something like, "Go to sleep, my little girl, we have had some fun. We sang some songs to you, and now your day is done."

Dad remained attentive as I grew older. For instance, the various times when my teeth hung by a thread, he yanked them out, put them under my pillow, and told me that the Tooth Fairy would visit me during the night. Then he kissed me on my forehead, eyes, and cheeks as he wished me sweet dreams. Fifty times a day, Dad would say to me, "I love you, Mush"—his and Mom's nickname for me—and he would hold me so tight. I was truly a "Daddy's little girl."

He found ways to make me feel special even in the most common experiences, like when he put me on his lap as he mowed the lawn, as if I were a princess. And in a classic rite of childhood passage that many people can relate to, Dad, along with Mom, taught me how to ride a bike, urging me to get back on it again and again after many falls.

Dad took me and my brothers on joy rides in his various cars as well. From his speakers he blared his music, from the British rock of the Beatles to the Southern rock of the Marshall Tucker Band and the folk and pop rock of Harry Chapin. I can still see him lying on our living room floor with his headphones on too, lost in music. All the songs that filled our home every day seeped into my soul and planted a love of music in me that would flower as I got older.

In some ways, our family life seemed idyllic. Dad would put his two pinky fingers under his tongue and whistle, signaling my brothers and me to ride our bikes back to our cul-de-sac to come home for dinner, which we shared together almost every night. As a family, we also regularly attended temple on the Jewish holidays and practiced our faith at home. I'll never forget Dad praying in his bedroom closet on Yom Kippur, the day of repentance and atonement, focused on asking God for forgiveness.

Mom and Dad wanted us kids to deeply understand our faith, so they sent us to Hebrew school twice a week. There we prayed and learned about the significance of our holidays, aspects of our religion, and how to read and write Hebrew. Dad extended those lessons and other teachings into our home. He used everyday real-life situations and movies to make his point. One day, he made me and my brothers sit down in the living room to watch *Mask*, a movie about a teen with a disfigured face. In *Mask*, a blind girl falls in love with the teen because he has a beautiful spirit. At the end of the movie, Dad explained to us one of its lessons: Never judge a book by its cover but instead fall in love with someone's heart.

Another movie Dad made us gather around the TV to watch showed the terrifying world of drug addicts. Dad had a very strong reason to scare us off from using drugs. At the time we watched that movie, the crack epidemic was in full swing in relatively nearby New York City.

While my brothers and I had loving parents, not every part of our family life was ideal, and a lot of that had to do with Dad. The truth is, as much as I loved him, I feared him too. For one, he wasn't always as nice as he should have been to Mom. I saw this play out at home. Mom and Dad would present a good example of how a romantic relationship could look—for instance, I fondly remember them dancing in the kitchen when they didn't think anyone was watching and hugging and kissing like people in love do—but ultimately, something would make Dad snap. The majority of the time, he seemed to be picking a fight with Mom. For example, he wished out loud that Mom would become a better cook and would speak her mind. In his Yiddish accent, he would plead with her to fight with him, to say something, anything. But she wouldn't.

I think the discord stemmed from the fact that my parents were very different from each other. Mom, a second-generation American, didn't identify with Dad's background. While members of his immediate family were suffering in the concentration camp, Mom's father was serving in the US Marines, in combat in Japan. That could not have been an easy experience for him, but by contrast, it was not the same as a family enduring the possibility that all of its members could die in a war.

Additionally, Mom's upbringing was cushier than Dad's. After returning from World War II, Mom's father became a New York City firefighter and married a woman who would work as a bookkeeper and school cafeteria worker. A few years after the war, Mom came along and her parents raised her in the North Bronx in a brand-new two-bedroom apartment in a middle-class area with Jewish, Italian, and Irish people. Meanwhile, my father's family lived in an old, outdated apartment in a heavily Jewish section of Washington Heights and experienced a harder life as a striving family struggling to assimilate into a new world.

Though Mom had an easier childhood, her dad subjected her and others in their household to the strict military lifestyle of order and service he had learned as a soldier in battle. In that regard, Mom and Dad shared a similarity: Both had strict parents who pushed them to succeed. Just as the discipline in Dad's household helped him move up in the world, the discipline Mom experienced at home served her well too, though in different ways. She earned good grades, didn't do drugs, except for trying pot once as a teen and disliking it, and hardly drank. She didn't smoke cigarettes either, something that Dad did all the time. But her upbringing also seemed to have made her quiet. I never heard her speak up for herself.

In our household, the biggest issue was money. Dad always complained to Mom about "all the bills." He threw chairs, slammed doors, and yelled at Mom to get her to respond. Once, he threw a chair so hard that he broke a part of the kitchen floor and put a large dent in our wall. I never saw him rough up Mom though, but the same could not be said for our dog. When he did his business on the floor, Dad would kick him and put his nose in it.

Sometimes, Dad also spanked my brothers when they didn't listen to him; but he never physically harmed me. Now, if he had lived to see me on drugs, I'm certain he would have beat the shit out of me. But here's the irony: I don't think I would have ever done drugs had Dad lived because I would have been too scared of him. I really feared him. When he rampaged, I hid in my closet and played with my dolls to calm down.

Dad set another bad example: He chain-smoked. And when his friends were over for poker night, all their cigar and cigarette smoke competed for air space.

Dad's rage and frustration resulted in high blood pressure, anxiety, and heart attacks.

I don't remember his age when he suffered his first coronary, but I remember what happened after he returned home from the hospital with a stent to improve blood flow to his heart.

The doctors had told him to stop smoking, yet after only a brief time giving up cigarettes after his heart attack, he began hiding them everywhere, from his cars to his home office, just like an alcoholic hides bottles.

Meanwhile, Mom was doing what she could to help him. She made the family healthy food, accompanied Dad to the gym to make sure he worked out, and urged him to quit smoking. But Dad didn't want to stop smoking, so he continued to do it.

One day at a restaurant, after a trip to the gym with Mom, Dad suffered a second heart attack. In the hospital that night, doctors put another stent in him. Overnight, Dad experienced a third heart attack and died two days after my youngest brother Eli's eleventh birthday.

Dad was forty-one.

The day Dad died, our house filled up with family members and neighbors. Within twenty-four hours, we held his service; in the Jewish religion, everything happens so fast.

I remember seeing a big building—a temple in Suffolk County, not far from our home. That's where my family attended services and my brothers and I went to Hebrew school. Many family members and friends gathered. I saw a closed wooden box. It held Dad. Someone opened the box to let my brothers see Dad for the last time, but because I was so young, Mom didn't let me look.

After the service, we headed to a Jewish cemetery. I watched as people lowered the box into the ground. After all was said and done, we drove home.

As family members gathered inside our house, I sat outside on the driveway pavement feeling confused. I knew that something had happened to my dad, but I didn't really understand that he wasn't coming back. His funeral was the first one I ever attended or the first one I remember. Relatives told me that Dad was in heaven, but my eight-year-old mind couldn't wrap itself around that. I didn't really know what death was.

After Dad died, the emotional and financial stability our family once knew disappeared. The only substantial thing that he left us was the house, which, thankfully, was paid off, but his many health issues had made it impossible for him to get life insurance. That, coupled with the fact that our two-parent household had suddenly become a one-person show, spelled a kind of doom for us.

We all grieved in our own ways. I cried a lot. Mom cried occasionally, but I never saw her really break down. My brothers, Eli and Noah, were angry and constantly fought each other.

From what I could see, my brothers hardly ever got in trouble for fighting. The family had lost its disciplinarian, a role that Mom was not cut out to fill. Maybe she couldn't step into the role because she was quiet by nature, or maybe this happened because she was now focused on finding work outside of the house. Mom had to become the sole breadwinner and figure out how to take care of three children, ages eight, eleven, and fourteen.

Not long after Dad died, the part-time nursing position Mom held, in a clinic, became a full-time gig. She made about $35,000 a year, but the job did not carry family benefits. Obviously, we couldn't live on Mom's income, so while she held that job, she continued to search for work until, about a year and a half later, she became a full-time nurse at a hospital and she left the clinic.

In the new job, Mom made around $55,000 annually—not a lot of money in an expensive state like New York, but at least the position paid more and included family benefits. In addition to that job, eventually she found part-time employment as a nurse at a doctor's office. The two jobs brought her total annual income up to about $75,000. She worked six days a week. My brothers and I were fortunate to see her for a few hours. Sometimes, we didn't see her at all.

We watched our mother struggle. We needed a roof and a boiler. We needed to get the house painted. We needed carpet. Mom couldn't afford any of these things. She wound up taking out a home equity loan to pay for them.

The family's bills overwhelmed Mom. Even though she was juggling two jobs, she could not afford to continue to pay for "luxuries" like temple and Hebrew school. She'd had to fork over about $1,000 a year to pay for me and my brothers to attend the school and about $125 for an adult ticket for High Holy Days celebrations. For someone who was struggling to cover the groceries and other basic necessities, she couldn't afford these extra bills. So our attendance at temple slacked off and, besides my family later participating in my bat mitzvah, the Jewish coming-of-age ceremony for girls, and in my youngest brother's bar mitzvah, our time there became part of history.

In the bargain, I lost some academically oriented friends. More important to me, I lost the sense of community at temple—celebrating holidays and the everyday joys of life with people we'd come to know and love over the years. In addition to Jewish traditions, we also lost our extended family. When Dad was living, every Sunday we had traveled to the Bronx to visit his youngest sister, a married woman who worked in a lingerie shop fitting women for bras. Additionally, Dad had often taken us to visit his first cousins, who lived nearby and upstate. But after his death, half of our family died because they all had a hard time looking at us . . . because we kids looked a lot like Dad.

The culmination of my family's financial struggles, hardly seeing Mom, and the gradual loss of our family identity finally caught up with me one cold day on my way to school.

As I stood outside, waiting for my turn to get on the school bus, I watched other parents walk their kids up to the bus and wish them a good day before saying bye. Then on my turn, as I walked up each bus step, it hit me hard that no parent stood on the sidewalk to wish me a great day. In that moment, I realized that my father was never coming back. Three years had passed since Dad's death. I was eleven years old. It took me that long to understand what death meant. Before this moment, I had looked at other people's dads and wondered where my father was.

That day, I realized just how alone, sad, and scared I felt.

I felt different because I did not have a dad.

I felt as if other people were looking at me with pity, and they were. I could read their feelings from how they carried themselves, how they sat in a chair, whether their leg was shaking, how they gave a hug, and the way they spoke with their hands or didn't. I could feel a person's sadness even if I wasn't looking at them because all I had to do was hear them talk. I sensed all of this even though I was only a child.

CHAPTER TWO

MY ADDICTIONS BEGIN

I believe the first sign of my addictive behavior reared its head when I was eight, some months before my father died.

It happened at a Rosh Hashanah dinner, observing the Jewish New Year. In the house of my dad's youngest sister, family members surrounded a table where we said a prayer before sipping wine to celebrate the holiday.

My aunt's husband gave me a wineglass. My parents noticed and allowed me to have a sip because of the special occasion. I distinctly remember the drink: Manischewitz, a Jewish wine. It tasted so good. When a family member turned their back—walked away from the table, went to the bathroom, got distracted while talking or eating—I'd pick up their glass and sip some of their drink. Doing this on the sly filled me with euphoria; I liked the taste of the wine, and I enjoyed getting away with something I knew I shouldn't be doing.

I believe the rush that wine gave me signaled that the tendency toward addiction lurked in my genes. If I'd only understood then how vulnerable I would be to using substances, I would never have taken that first sip.

I think I next drank at age eleven. It happened at a New Year's Eve party that my brothers threw at home while Mom spent time out with her friends. By this point, she was trying to get her personal life back together and was dating a lot. At the party, I stood at our kitchen table with some guys who were playing a game of beer pong. They were throwing a small ball into a cup of beer, which the opponent had to drink if the ball landed in the cup. While the guys played and drank, they gave me drinks too and laughed at me as I got tipsy.

I drank a few Coors Lights, which made me drunk. Finally, I lay on the couch and fell asleep in the midst of a big, crazy party full of wasted kids.

The party ended after one of the drunk partygoers, a big, muscular dude, fell through a thin glass shower door, sending shards all over an upstairs bathroom. The crash woke me up and prompted my oldest brother, Noah, to send everyone home immediately. I don't remember how we later explained the shattered shower door to Mom, but I do remember that those Coors Lights *fully* turned on the ignition that the Manischewitz had first turned a half notch three years earlier.

At age twelve, I drank again, and it was on. It happened in the summer while I stayed with maternal relatives in Florida. I stole cigarettes and alcohol from a family member, hid them in a backpack, and hung out at the movies with a girl with whom I shared my stash. When I came home, none of my relatives said a word to me about the alcohol on my breath. No one disciplined me for drinking, so I didn't think I was doing anything wrong . . . so I kept drinking.

I was depressed as a preteen, though I didn't realize it. Every day I walked into my house I could feel Dad's presence, but not being able to see or hear him was tearing me apart. Then, of course, Mom wasn't home much. I missed both of my parents.

Something funny was happening though. When I drank a bit too much, these sad feelings would disappear. I liked that, and soon I would discover that illegal drugs numbed these feelings even more.

Drugs were so easy to get because they were everywhere, including our neighborhood. At age twelve, I smoked pot, the first drug I ever used, with my fifteen-year-old brother, Eli. Eli got it for free from friends or paid for it with the little money he made painting houses. He'd buy it from a dealer not far from our home or get rides from his friends, who drove about an hour from our suburb to Brooklyn and Harlem to get high. The pot didn't wreck his wallet. It cost about ten dollars for a little more than a dime-sized amount.

Smoking pot became a habitual thing for Eli and me to do when Mom wasn't home. Occasionally, we also smoked it with Noah on his breaks from school; he had started attending college out of state by this time, so he wasn't around a lot.

With such easy access to drugs and alcohol, by age thirteen, if I could drink it, pop it, or smoke it, I did. It all made me forget that Dad was gone. I thought, *Yes, this is the answer to all of my problems. This is it!* No adult was telling me otherwise. I thought, *This is what's going to make my pain stop.*

Eli and I would smoke pot in his room then blow it out the window to reduce our chances of Mom getting a whiff and putting two and two together. Once, Mom came home unexpectedly while we were getting high. So much for blowing smoke out the window. The smell of marijuana filled the house enough for Mom to smell it. She knew exactly what it was. Also, she already knew that Eli was doing drugs and in fact had already put him in therapy for that and for anger problems. On this particular day, she blamed him for the pot. She didn't point a finger at me.

One time, however, Mom grounded me for an entire weekend because I had come home smelling like alcohol. I don't recall her ever punishing me again for drinking, but then again, she later claimed that she didn't realize I was doing that. Maybe she thought I had stopped drinking after that one time she smelled alcohol on my breath.

Of course, I also risked Mom grounding me for doing drugs. Whatever, I took the risk because they made me feel *so* good and made everything, including myself, look better too. For a kid who was not comfortable in her own skin, this was heaven. At thirteen, I was big for my age—much bigger than the other girls in school—with what I thought were big boobs, big feet, and a big nose. I was 130 pounds and already my mother's height, five foot six, with an inch more to grow. Also, I had to wear glasses, which I hated, so most of the time I took them off in class because I didn't want to be called four eyes. I didn't think I looked good, though other people begged to differ, and I didn't think I was skinny enough. But on drugs, I felt like a beauty queen.

As my drug use took root, I was attending a middle school in a nice neighborhood with big, fancy houses. Our school looked rich too, set on a campus with athletic fields. Like any school, it had the nerds, the jocks, the beauty queens, and the druggies. Quickly, I fell into the latter clique. Sometimes, we cut classes to smoke pot, which kids could buy from a classmate who hung out on the fields near the bleachers, or we smoked it after school while listening to the likes of Nirvana and Nine Inch Nails on CD at somebody's house. It was the early 1990s.

Busing routes had split me up from many of my elementary school friends who were good students. Most of them had wound up at different middle schools. The few who were going to my school weren't in my classes, and we didn't share the same lunch period either. On weekends, I tried to get together with them to ice skate or go to the movies, but slowly but surely we weren't hanging out any longer. I was spending more time with my new friends, the ones who smoked pot and drank. I didn't realize it, but I was setting myself up for academic failure.

My smoking, drinking, cutting classes, and refusal to wear my eyeglasses resulted in a perfect brew of poor grades. A learning disability plagued me too, which did not help things. I struggled with a short-term memory and comprehension problem and found it hard to focus. A crazy noise constantly screamed in my head. It prevented me from concentrating on my schoolwork.

My disability left me feeling dumb and "not good enough." Once, a teacher became so frustrated with me that he shouted, "What are you, stupid or something? Why can't you get this?" I told him that I just didn't understand.

When I attended elementary school, Mom recognized I had a problem comprehending words, so she took extra time to help me learn how to read. She put a ruler or a piece of paper under each line in a book or assignment to assist me in following along. During my middle school years, she continued this practice. But I needed a lot more help, which I did not find in my new school, where there was only one teacher for about every thirty students.

My learning disability eroded my self-esteem. The only things that helped me feel better about myself were the alcohol and drugs.

The middle school years are some of the toughest for all kids. We go through a lot of changes, physical and emotional, as we begin to turn into adults. Even when geography doesn't separate us from our old elementary school friends, other things might, like physically developing slower, or faster, and having new interests, like, say, the opposite sex.

Because so many of my old elementary friends wound up in other schools, I'll never know for sure what, if any, positive influence they might have had on me had we attended the same middle school. But I can definitely say that I gained a new best friend, Lannie, and neither one of us was a good influence on the other.

Lannie, an Italian-American brunette who loved to dye her hair reddish brown, was in several of my classes, and before I knew it, we were hanging out every day. We lived within walking distance of each other. After school, either Lannie hung out at my house, or I hung out at hers. The couple of times I got in trouble at school, I was with Lannie cutting class, which resulted in in-school suspension for us.

My friendship with Lannie showed that it's not only kids from single-parent households who are vulnerable to drugs. Lannie came from a two-parent home, but that didn't stop drugs and alcohol from touching her life. At her house, it was actually *easier* to get these things. She and I would take her mom's liquor out of the cabinet and drink it. We'd steal her mom's tranquilizers from the cabinet in the main bathroom and take them too.

When her mom realized what we were doing, she lectured us to stop stealing her pills but she didn't rat me out to my mom and she didn't punish Lannie. In fact, Lannie's mom even bought us alcohol a few times. The fact is, she related to Lannie more as a friend, not really as a mother. Hell, they smoked pot together. Lannie's mom seemed to let her do whatever she wanted.

There is no excuse for her mom's behavior, but you have to remember, this was the '90s. Fact is, New York City had the reputation of being the drug capital of the world. And that's exactly how my little section of Long Island felt too—after all, it was not that far from the influences of the big bad city. In my town, it felt like everyone was doing drugs, from kids to parents. It felt like nobody had a care in the world. It was all about doing drugs.

It wasn't just lax adult supervision at home that got me and my friend into trouble. Adult strangers enabled us too. Lannie and I could get alcohol just by hanging out in front of a neighborhood 7-Eleven. We'd use our feminine wiles, batting our eyelashes and showing off cleavage in tank tops, as we asked attractive guys in their twenties to buy us drinks. We'd give them our money and tell them what we wanted. Lannie, all of about five feet tall and around 100 pounds, didn't look older than thirteen, but I did, and that's all we needed. With my height, makeup, and revealing clothes, I could pass for eighteen. Lannie and I had no problems getting alcohol, and no, guys did not try anything on us. They'd just come out of the store to give us our drinks and our change and, after a little flirting, they'd drive off.

At that time in my life, hanging out with Lannie was everything to me. With her, I experienced a kind of spacey, free feeling as we traveled around the neighborhood or lay on her bedroom floor laughing and being silly. The two of us just loved each other. Spending time with Lannie made me feel like I was connected in some deep way to another human being, unlike how I felt at home. Lannie made me feel like I wasn't alone.

I didn't see her as a bad friend at all. In reality, we caused trouble in each other's lives, but I didn't recognize that at the time.

I was a free spirit, the life of the party, sarcastic. I danced around, joked a lot, made people laugh. I talked a lot in class and didn't pay much attention. I tried not to take life too seriously. Lannie and I shared that view. After all, if I had learned anything from my dad's death it's that we aren't getting out of this thing alive, so we may as well have fun and enjoy every moment.

So, my adventures with Lannie began to extend beyond drugs. We went to house parties, where the parents weren't home, and we drank and got stoned and had oral sex with boys, giving it and receiving it. Everyone in our multiracial and multireligious clique was doing it. There was no penetration; honestly, that scared me. I was still just thirteen.

We were all kind of drunk and stoned on pot and trying to figure out what felt good. My gut told me that I was doing something wrong and shouldn't be involved. That would become a pattern: going against my instinct to do the right thing. I would later see this as a battle of wills—my will to do wrong and God's will, which always seemed to be the exact opposite of what I was thinking to do. In these years, unfortunately, my will always won.

As you can see, I had no direction in life and neither did the kids in my clique. Their issues were similar to mine: having parents with problems, living in single-parent homes, having parents who weren't home much. However, I saw them as the "cool kids," and I went along with them. I wanted them to accept me, and I also wanted to be popular, things that most kids identify with. And while I held the line at oral sex, at some point, I began to feel that maybe I should go further to really "get in" with this crowd. That's because one day after school, Lannie revealed to me that she'd had sex.

Lannie and I were sitting on her bed as she told me about her experience. She said that it had hurt a little bit and then it had started to feel good. She seemed excited and happy as she bragged about it and acted like she was cool because she had done it. She pretty much told me that I should do it too. For the first time, Lannie made me feel uncomfortable.

I felt confused too.

Lannie made sex sound like it was not a big deal, but I thought that it was supposed to be more special than she described it; special, like movie-star sex. I also thought I was supposed to be older when I did it and be in love. I really felt like I should wait for that special someone, yet I wondered if something was wrong with me because I hadn't done it.

I mean, that's what Lannie seemed to imply.

In my middle school years, I'm sure people, both around me and on television and the radio, promoted messages about doing the right thing—not doing drugs and not having sex. But I heard none of it. I didn't talk about—and I ignored—a lot of the thoughts swirling through my mind too.

I also ignored my emotions. I didn't say much about my dad, my mom, or my real feelings, and my closest friend picked up on that. Lannie used to ask me why I didn't talk about my dad. And when she came to my house, she asked why my mom wasn't home. I'd tell

Lannie that I didn't want to talk about my dad—it hurt too much. I'd tell her that my mom was working or out with her friends.

Subconsciously, I was following Mom's lead. I wasn't talking about my feelings.

After Dad died, Mom had become the epitome of stoicism. She wanted to be strong for us, she said and added that that's how she needed to be for us. In general, whether it had to do with Dad or anything else, I never saw Mom get really emotional. For instance, when I got my period for the first time, a day after my thirteenth birthday, I sought her out to share the news. She laughed and said, "I'm not ready for this." Then she took me upstairs to her bathroom to show me where she kept the pads. She didn't show me how to put a pad on. That was the extent of her acknowledgment of that momentous day in my life.

Mom seemed to have suppressing her feelings down to a science. Seemingly unlike her, however, I needed help to keep mine at bay. So, I kept using drugs to tamp them down. Other kids always thought I was happy, but really I was just high all the time. I didn't know how to be happy or sad or disappointed or how to feel any kind of joy, anger, fear, or confidence without using drugs. The drugs were hiding a shaky, insecure little girl who was crying out for help. I was the girl who could be in a room full of people and feel completely and utterly alone. Drugs made me forget that.

Unfortunately for me, the more drugs I used, the more horrific situations I got into, which I will elaborate on soon. I descended into a deeper and deeper hole of despair and destruction. I didn't even realize what I was hiding from.

Today, I know that I was hiding from my family, hiding from feelings of being alone and empty inside. I was hiding from my mother all while wanting to connect with her and have her attention. She wanted us to see her as a strong woman, but I needed something more from her. I needed to see her break down to show us that that was okay to do.

By age fourteen, I was using drugs almost every day and thought I was having fun. In reality, I was becoming more lost.

I paid for the drugs with my jobs babysitting and at an ice cream shop. Ironically, I look back at these jobs and sort of smile because they remind me of Mom. She would always tell me and my brothers that we needed to know how to provide for ourselves. To me, she would say, "Never depend on a man. Always hold your own and stand on your own feet." She *showed* me the lesson through how she lived and raised me. For instance, after she helped me buy a car in my later teen years, she insisted that I pay for my own insurance. After she bought me a cell phone, she made it clear that I had to pay my own phone bills.

Mom insisted that my brothers and I do our share to keep the house running as well. Early on, we learned how to do our own laundry and clean our own rooms. We took turns dusting, mopping, and cleaning other areas of the house too. These skills came in handy when, at one point, Eli began to bring home every animal in the world. Our "guests" included stray dogs, cats, a ferret, and even once three ducks, who pooped all over the house!

In addition to my jobs, I paid for drugs with spending money Mom gave me. I also got them for free when I made out with guys. They knew if they gave us girls drugs we would probably let them kiss and grope us. Half the time, these guys were so strung out that they didn't even realize they were giving their drugs away.

Soon, my ability to pay for drugs and my ever-widening circle of druggie friends led me to snort cocaine for the first time. It happened at Lannie's house with her boyfriend, Vinny, and a friend named Josh. Josh looked at me and said he didn't think I should try coke because he thought I would like it too much. I was like, "Get the fuck out of here. Give it to me then." Liking it too much was the point. He fought me, but I gave back verbally as good as I got. I broke him down. He gave me the coke.

Josh was right. As soon I put that first line up my nose, it was over. At just fourteen years old, I absolutely loved how light, confident, and energetic cocaine made me feel. That same night, I arrived home to find Eli with Ian, a local drug dealer and good friend, sitting at our coffee table hunched over lines of coke spread out like gleaming white snow. I had to have some more. I begged Eli, who didn't want me to get started on the stuff. But I convinced him that I'd already snorted coke, so he relented.

Once, I brought a bunch of coke to Lannie's house. We broke it out into lines on a table in her bedroom. Vinny came over and flipped out when he saw us snorting it. Then he literally flipped the table, and powder flew everywhere. He told me it was okay if I wanted to fuck up my life but that he wouldn't let me do it to Lannie. Then he kicked me out of her house.

CHAPTER THREE

LITERALLY "HIGH" SCHOOL

School is supposed to be where you learn and apply yourself for a shot at college or trade school and a bright career. However, my high school, which I'll call James High, seemed to be the place where you learned how to become a drug addict. As far as I'm concerned, it was literally a "high" school. Before I get too far, for those wondering how I even made it there with all my middle school shenanigans, it happened because my teachers just passed me along.

Something like 1,000 or more kids attended racially mixed James, a school located in what looked like a rich neighborhood. On my way there, I'd stare at what appeared to be million-dollar homes surrounding it and wonder, *What the hell do people have to do to make this kind of money?* Kids drove BMWs and shiny Mustangs to James while teens like me and Lannie took the bus.

The moment I would arrive to school, I could bump into someone either outside, by the lockers, or in the cafeteria selling drugs. It felt like everyone was either selling or doing them, from the athletes to the nerds . . . and sometimes, even the staff.

Once, I saw kids bribe the security guard with a bottle of vodka to let them out of school early. They would cut class to hang out in the baseball dugouts or in the woods behind the baseball fields to smoke pot. Another time, someone dropped acid into a teacher's coffee. She started acting weird and seeing stuff.

The drugs on offer at James High included angel dust, cocaine, special k, mescaline, ecstasy, pot, and acid, a lot of which was going around because acid was cheap, about ten dollars for one drop on a small piece of paper. I can't even remember everything else. If the dealer, typically a fellow high school student, didn't have drugs on him, you could order them for home delivery. I had it even easier because Eli, also a James student, was friends with some of our school's dealers. All I had to do was be his sister to get my drugs of choice. So, my freshman year, my drug repertoire expanded from coke and pot to all the other drugs available at school.

For about a gram, prices ranged from ten dollars to as high as sixty dollars depending on the drug, its purity level, and where you bought it. Drugs were always cheaper, and better, in New York City than on Long Island, but being high school students, we couldn't always make it into the city.

At James, I made many friends and partied with everybody. I didn't discriminate. My parents didn't raise me that way. I looked at everyone the same. If you were getting high—black, white, Latino, Asian, Jewish, Christian, Catholic, or Muslim—I was hanging with you. If you weren't getting high, I was still hanging with you. I didn't care what you looked like or how cool, popular, pretty, hot, skinny or heavy, gay or straight you were. If you were partying, well there was Marsha with a smile.

Having so many schoolmate acquaintances made it easy to cash in on favors to take advantage of James's lax culture. Sometimes, the security guard would look away or other students would lie for me so I could cut class to get high. I was leaving school to do that all the time. Friends would be like, "Marsha, let's do (fill in the blank—you name it, we did it)." And off we'd go to the baseball dugouts or the football field bleachers. If you were down, I was down. I was like, "Let's do this. You want to get high—okay, cool."

The kids in the drug scene at school all knew the hot party spots, the places we could hang out in and do whatever we wanted because the parents weren't often home. Once, at some student's house party not far from my house, I took six-foot bong hits of dust and pot mixed together and, not having any real sense of what I was doing, I attempted to jump off a balcony. Eli, who was at the party too, remembers that he grabbed my arm just in time and pulled me off the ledge, then I stumbled back into the house and laughed everything off.

As it happens, my house earned a reputation for being one of the best party spots and a place where teens crashed after partying and doing drugs elsewhere. At times, Mom would return home from work or one of her dates to find something like ten kids passed out on her living room furniture. That was a normal Saturday. Normal!

Eli and I let our mother, the woman who barely touched alcohol and whose "drug use" had consisted of trying pot one time as a teen, believe that we were just hosting slumber parties. We lied a lot to her, and she largely accepted what we said, though she didn't completely trust Eli. After all, she had made him see a therapist for his drug and anger issues. But with Mom out so often at work or on dates, she didn't have much of a way to check Eli's and my stories or to control us. That gave us too much time to get into far more trouble.

Unfortunately for me, I never got sick or had any bad trips on any of the drugs I took. I hear that a lot of drugs make "normal" people sick the first time. If that had happened to me, maybe I wouldn't have continued using them. But because that wasn't the case, I'd keep on experimenting, and that would come back to bite me in the ass in a big way . . .

The very first time I took acid, I was smoking pot and drinking too. I was not in the right frame of mind, and I was in the wrong place at the wrong time.

It all happened at Luke's house, the most popular party hangout for kids in my neighborhood. Luke, twenty, still lived at home with his well-off parents and was entitled and screwed up; I was a ninth grader, a kid trying to fit in.

I know I'm responsible for doing drugs, but Luke took extreme advantage of the situation, one that I couldn't count on my friends to help me get out of because they helped get me into it.

Here's what happened:

Lannie and a guy were having sex on the floor in Luke's bedroom while Luke and I hung out in the room on the "sidelines" doing drugs. Then Lannie and this guy began encouraging Luke and me to have sex. Lannie had been telling me to "get it over with" ever since she'd lost her virginity. She had told me that once I lost mine too, I'd be relieved.

On this night, she and her friend were kind of chanting at me and this man to "do it." As the peer pressure to go all the way swirled around me in my altered state, it happened.

Let me be clear: Luke raped me. There is no other way to describe a twenty-year-old man having sex with a fourteen-year-old. That's how I lost my virginity. I knew that it was happening, but I was not in a physical or mental state to verbally say "yes" or "no" to the sexual act. After the horror ended, with Lannie and her guy friend looking on, I walked into the hallway bathroom. I felt dirty as I looked into the mirror at a face I suddenly didn't recognize. Then I experienced this awful, uncomfortable feeling as I wiped myself and found blood on the toilet paper. I threw up.

Later that night, Lannie's mom picked Lannie and me up from Luke's. On the way home, I stared out the car window and said nothing. Today, I wonder how many young girls get drugged and date raped every day and don't say anything because they don't understand what exactly happened to them. I don't know about you, but I had always thought rape had to be brutal and violent.

That night, I found out that that isn't always so; but at the time, I didn't accept that I had been raped.

The day after the party, I went to school and learned that Lannie and her guy friend had been telling people what happened between Luke and me. "People" included Eli. With disgust and disappointment, he told me what he'd heard. The look on his face wrenched my heart. I had no words.

The night of the rape, and for days, months, and years later, I didn't talk to anyone about it. Honestly, it was much easier to live in denial. I wanted to forget it, so I buried it deep within me and took more drugs.

Years later, a boyfriend told me about the bad experiences that had made him become an addict, then he asked me about my addiction triggers. I shared with him many things, but after I told him about that night with Luke, he stopped me. "You were raped, and you're fucked up because of it," he said. That was the first time anyone called it "rape."

That life-changing conversation made me realize that I had been raped a bunch of times after Luke. It had all happened during active addiction, especially when I was high on special k, a hallucinogen that's known as a date rape drug. I had tried to push boys off of me, but I couldn't. Additionally, many times after passing out from the drug, I had come to only to find that my jeans were off and my private area felt sore—classic signs of being taken advantage of while unconscious.

After being raped, some people become introverted sexually. I became the opposite. It's like I changed overnight. I couldn't be alone. I couldn't be without a boyfriend, and if I didn't have a boyfriend, I had to be having sex with someone. It didn't matter if I liked the boy. You see, other kids had slapped me with a bad reputation as the girl who had "put out," and now, with my new promiscuous behavior, I was, unconsciously, making sure that reputation stuck. Meanwhile,

Luke remained superpopular, the guy from a rich family who lived in the best party house in the neighborhood. I even went back there. Nothing happened between Luke and me again, though I can't say the same for what happened between me and other boys elsewhere later.

At this point in my life, I believed that all guys just wanted sex, so that's what I gave them—we had sexual intercourse—despite the fact that everything about "real" sex, which I saw as being different from oral sex, scared me. Getting pregnant scared me. Sexually transmitted diseases scared me.

Before I began having intercourse, I hadn't really known anything about it besides what other kids had told and shown me and what I had learned in health class or seen in the movies. Mom had talked to me about how my body would change during puberty, but she had never talked to me about sex. Fortunately, I had learned enough from other kids to know that I needed to use condoms, which I did. The boys always seemed to have them in their wallet or a pocket.

The fact is, of the teens I knew, I was far from the only one having sex with numerous partners. Meanwhile, though my promiscuity was rooted in the incident with Luke, my drug use was exacerbating it and I think drugs, ecstasy in particular, played a role in me and so many other kids having so much sex so young. Ecstasy was fairly cheap, anywhere from fifteen to twenty dollars a pill, depending on the dealer. Many of us were out of our minds on the stuff.

I can't speak for the other teens, but sex became another drug for me. It let me pretend that everything was good. I thought if a boy wanted me then I must be beautiful and sexy and hot. I liked feeling that way. I also thought that if I had sex with these boys that maybe one day one of them would become my boyfriend; but that never happened.

My self-esteem was in the toilet, and I didn't want to feel alone. I was still struggling with Dad's death and Mom's absence, so I kept having sex to fill a void. Anything that felt good in the moment, I settled for it, even though my gut was telling me that what I was doing was wrong. I would get this knot in my stomach right before the act. I felt dirty inside, yet I also felt like I didn't know how to stop. Sex totally felt like an addiction, like what I experienced on drugs. My heart would race. I would feel excited. I would feel anxious, and then I would crash. My life was spinning out of control. I felt like I had absolutely no way out. I didn't feel like I could talk to anyone, so I didn't.

CHAPTER FOUR

PASSING THROUGH LIFE

The '90s in New York provided many party opportunities for a messed-up kid like me to get into trouble. I'm talking about the rave scene, a phenomenon that, for many people, defines the decade. Techno music poured from clubs and pop-up party spots as teens disappeared into their own la-la lands taking ecstasy and other drugs.

Raves flourished in my area. Friends in my neighborhood threw rave-type parties at their homes, and a real rave club was just about a ten-minute drive from my house. I hit that one on the regular, dancing on the speakers, sucking on strawberry-flavored lollipops, one of my favorite candies, thinking I was cool. I never got carded because I looked like an adult in my typical ensemble of tight jeans, boots, belly-button-baring tank top, black beanie hat, black eyeliner and mascara, and lipstick. I topped off my party look with sparkles on my face and glitter all over my body. The other ravers, tank-top-wearing girls and T-shirted boys, typically wore really big "counterculture" baggy jeans called JNCO, short for "Judge None Choose One."

At the club, I'd find my way outside to a trippy looking bus behind it. It sat next to an outside bar where people got high and made out. When I disappeared for hours at the club, Mom thought I was sleeping over at a friend's house. In reality, I was popping ecstasy, smoking dust and pot, drinking, you name it, all night at the rave. I'd snort huge rails of special k too, so I'd pass out at these parties and, again and again, wake up with my jeans down or disheveled and with a tender feeling between my legs.

❧

My adventures in the rave scene extended beyond Long Island. I liked some of the more aggressive clubs in Manhattan and Brooklyn, as did Eli. He or a friend would drive us into one of the boroughs or we'd take the train to a rave that happened regularly in an abandoned warehouse in Brooklyn or to other clubs in Manhattan. After clubbing, I'd hang out in parks with the drag queens or guys I had met at the clubs. I remember tripping out on drugs at a park with some guys, looking up at the stars, and seeing the beautiful purple clouds.

Many of my memories of this time are fairly benign, but one memory stands out. One New Year's Eve, hundreds of people packed the warehouse in Brooklyn, including dozens of students from my high school. I was popping ecstasy, smoking pot, drinking alcohol, and doing whatever else partygoers passed around. I'd come with Eli and a bunch of other friends, but somehow I had become separated from them.

There I was dancing to the other side of the warehouse, a hot mess surrounded by sweaty bodies gyrating to the techno music, when suddenly the lights flickered. Men in uniform with badges rushed the club. It was the cops! It was a raid! As I looked around, half out of my mind, I did not see my brother and friends anywhere.

I made it out of the club without the cops picking me up. Then I searched frantically for my brother, but I had no luck finding him and his friends. Finally, I bumped into some dudes from Brooklyn who agreed to take me home; but in the next second, one of my brother's friends, Layne, spotted me and soon Eli and I were reunited in a hug. Layne stood on the sidelines saying, "You have no idea how much your brother loves you." Having seen the worry on Eli's face, I knew that Layne spoke the truth.

That raid inspired me to limit my time on the rave scene. I wanted to spend my money on getting high more than I wanted to spend it on a rave ticket anyway. I preferred to snort lines of coke for days at someone's house. Plus, I wasn't a fan of techno music, which was a staple of the clubs. I was a rock 'n roll girl. I loved Alice in Chains, Nirvana, Tracy Chapman, Rage Against the Machine, Nine Inch Nails, Soundgarden, and Sublime, just to name a few. I identified with their lyrics about drugs, love, loss, fear, death, survival, pain, wanting to die, fighting to live and for your life, fighting for what you believe in. Their music eased my conflict-ridden soul.

Ironically, many of my favorite '90s musicians later died from overdoses and suicide. That definitely says something about that harsh decade.

With all my focus on drugs, school fell to the bottom of my priority list. Consequently, my unconscious efforts to destroy my high school career were proving successful.

In addition to C's and D's, I earned F's. Mom had hired a tutor to help me with math, my worst subject, but I showed no progress. I received in-school tutoring too and Mom sat down to help me with homework a few times, but I demonstrated no desire to learn. Her efforts to help me do well, coupled with my poor attitude and a string of poor grades, frustrated her.

My grades continued to tank, and as they did, I didn't confide in Mom much or show her my report card. I didn't want her to know how bad things were. I didn't want to add to her stress. She was already caving under the weight of my lack of progress and the pressures of her single-parent life.

I didn't manage to hide everything from Mom though. Administrators let her know that I was skipping school. When she learned about this, she gave me a talking-to but she didn't punish me.

Maybe she felt doing that would be futile since she would probably not be home to enforce the punishment anyway.

At any rate, my school performance nosedived. Ultimately, between the bad grades, bad behavior, and school absences, I frustrated administrators too. In my sophomore year, they kicked me out of school.

Administrators forced me to enroll in an offsite alternative education program where my classmates would include messed-up kids with drug or anger problems. By this time, Lannie and I were no longer friends—a deep rift had developed after what had happened with Luke—and I wasn't leaving behind any other real friends either.

When school officials told Mom I would be sent to a special program, she didn't say much. She already knew a lot about it; at some point after I started going to James, Eli had been kicked out of our school and sent to this same program. He had finished it early and graduated. Now, it was my turn to go. Mom told me she believed I had to attend because I had cut classes.

Over the course of a little over two years, I attended three schools that housed the program. The first one was the opposite of my high school, a small building set in a struggling Suffolk County neighborhood with small houses, broken fences, and some untended lawns. I remember the school having only one hallway. In all, it seemed that about thirty kids were enrolled.

In the program, I met some other kids who were just as messed up as me or worse. Their infractions included drug dealing, using drugs, cutting classes, and fighting. Though there might have been some kids there who wanted to get things right, none that I knew seemed too keen about getting their acts together or thought at all about consequences, including me.

On the bus ride to school, we typically smoked dust blunts, a hollowed-out cigar filled with pot and angel dust, right in front of the driver, a thin, long-gray-haired old lady who wore blue jeans with an elastic waistband. We'd make fun of her, calling her an "old druggie" under our breath. She'd tell us to stop "smoking that funny stuff" on the bus, but we never listened because we had no respect for her . . . or just about anyone else. We kept lighting up, and she never pushed things any further.

Maybe she was scared to report us because of what she thought we might do to her. She'd drop us off at school like nothing had happened, and we'd be on our way to playing volleyball for the school day. We'd get high on campus too. Some of us would take acid or do a couple of lines of coke in the bathroom. I don't recall anyone ever patting us down to check for drugs.

The alternative program was a breeze. It seemed like we were guaranteed to pass our courses just by attending it. Okay, so I was kind of exaggerating when I said we played sports there all day. Yeah, we also took classes, like English and math, but we received minimal work, just enough to finish in school without having to have homework.

At one point, one of my teachers told me that I was too smart to be in the program and that if I just stopped using drugs—something I admitted to staff I was doing after some months of being enrolled—and applied myself, I could re-enter the regular high school. It sounded so easy: Just stop using drugs and apply myself. But it wasn't simple at all.

By this point, I couldn't "just stop." I was no longer using drugs—they were using me, though I didn't realize that. I craved them. I had a problem that I could not easily solve. I was a kid silently screaming for help, but I couldn't receive it because I wasn't willing to help myself.

The program required us to visit individually with counselors in the building. Several times a week, we talked with them in group sessions too. At the time, I saw them as people just getting paid to do a job, not as people who cared. Today, I know that they in fact cared a great deal. But because of my attitude at the time, it took me a few months to open up to them about my drug use.

Unfortunately, the information I shared with the counselors did not wind up helping me.

When I finally revealed some things about my drug escapades to them, they turned right around and told my mother. After that, I never told them anything about my drug use again.

The day they called Mom, I arrived home to an inquisition. She sat me down at the kitchen table and expressed concern. She asked if what they had said was true. I looked her straight in the eyes and lied. "Mom, I smoked pot and I drank once, and I tried ecstasy once. That's it." She seemed to believe me. I don't recall her pursuing the issue any further. There was no demand for a drug test, no fight, no grounding, no nothing. I was free to do what I wanted.

The next day at school, a teacher asked me what my mom had said the previous night. I told him that she had asked me some questions but didn't say much after that. Disbelief colored his face.

Mom was a good mother in many ways, but in this area of my life, she failed.

Over the years, Mom *had* been there for me in her way. She took me to my first concert, to hear the Motown sound of The Temptations and The Four Tops, a show I'll never forget. She took me to numerous Broadway plays and shopping for clothes too. We had a lot of fun. I was close enough to her that I once lectured her about making a decision regarding a guy; she was torn over two of them, and I told her to pick one. But that's all I can really remember.

Mom and I just didn't have an emotional relationship. Later, in my twenties, after my drug use was too obvious to deny, she told me that she hadn't known that I was on drugs when I was a teen. I don't believe that's true. I believe that she just wanted so desperately to believe that her little girl was okay.

That was the problem, hers and mine: We were both in denial about my addiction.

While caring adults genuinely wanted to see me succeed, my addiction had me so twisted up that I couldn't see, or care, about my future. Momentary pleasure was what I was about. I ignored opportunities to grow intellectually in the alternative program, but I welcomed the chance to experience a sexual growth of sorts there.

It all started on the volleyball court. It, or rather *she*, had a name: Holly.

While playing volleyball, my eyes fell on hers for the first time. She captivated me. In that moment, I felt like I'd known her my entire life. She would become my first girl kiss, my first girl partner, my first girl everything. She would become my best friend and girlfriend.

Starting from our days in the alternative program, Holly and I had sex with each other and did all types of drugs together. For almost half a dozen years, we were almost inseparable, though we were never in a committed relationship.

That said, I don't remember much about how my sexual relationship with Holly began. I was on so many drugs during my first time with her that much of the experience is a blur; but I remember kissing her and liking it. Everything was softer; her lips were softer than a boy's as were her hugs.

I believe, during that first time, that Holly and I had a threesome with a guy. Besides liking Holly's kisses and hugs, I felt nothing more. I had no emotions and was really more just going *through* motions. Every time I slept with Holly again, I was on drugs.

My experience with Holly left me wondering if I was bisexual. During my time with her, I had a few romantic liaisons with girls that consisted of just kissing and above-the-waist stuff. Several years after being with Holly, however, I had a handful of satisfying full-on sexual experiences with women, but they never became relationships. These encounters always followed the same pattern: I would run to a woman after a man hurt me. I did this to fill an emotional void, hoping that a woman might be the answer to my romantic aspirations because a man hadn't fulfilled them. While I had no problems attracting men, I never seemed to be the right type for the lesbians I slept with though. But I can't put it all on them. I never caught real feelings for any of these women.

I passed through my alternative-school years with no boundaries around myself, drugwise and sexwise. I continued to snort huge rails of special k, which made me pass out at parties a few times and continue to get raped, though I was still not seeing it as rape. To me, it was all just part of the lifestyle I had chosen. It was all about fun and, ya know, good times.

Not only did I allow people to take advantage of me, I crossed other people's boundaries too, which included one episode of violence. At a party, Holly and I were making out in a room when suddenly a woman exploded in on us and threatened me for sleeping with her boyfriend; in my defense, the guy had told me he was single. Also, I hadn't slept with him—I'd just made out with him.

I didn't care for the woman's accusation, so I attacked her. I grabbed her by the hair then dragged her down the stairs. At the bottom, I punched her over and over. It took several guys and a girl to pull me off of her. I didn't seriously injure her, but I scared myself and everyone around me that night. I never got into a fight with a woman again.

Though I hadn't slept with that woman's boyfriend, however, I certainly slept with others'. I didn't care if a guy was in a relationship. If he wanted to hook up with me and I was wasted on drugs, I'd do it. I wasn't the greatest person in the world in that way. For instance, this girl Julie hated me because I had had sex with her boyfriend and then, after her breakup with that guy, I started smoking with her new boyfriend and he "liked" me too and one thing led to another...

I hate to say it, but I also had sex with a cousin's boyfriend. I got high and drunk with him, and then it happened. My cousin found out and told some family members (Mom wasn't on this trip and as far as I know, never got word). Of course, I denied the accusation, because, well, that's what I did. I lied about everything because God forbid I tell the truth and be held accountable. I just didn't think straight. Years later, after getting clean, I owned up to my cousin about my behavior and offered an apology. Thankfully, she accepted it.

Then there was the college campus visit I made with a male friend. I accompanied him to the school to see an old classmate of his. While on campus, we all wound up at a rave-type party, and before I knew it, guys were giving me all kinds of drugs. I don't remember what the hell else happened at the party, and I don't think what they say happened actually happened, but who knows.

Supposedly, I rolled on the floor with one guy—others say it was five guys—and I don't remember having sex with him and definitely not the other guys, though people say I did. They say I did this in front of everyone. The only thing I know for sure is that whatever happened that night made me look pretty bad because some of the people at that party never spoke to me again.

What I *do* remember about that awful experience is what happened afterward with a guy I'll call Mason. At some point during that night, he told me, "Marsha, you have a problem. You may want to get help." Mason seemed to genuinely care. He didn't try to hook up with me. He didn't judge me. Yes, he was one of the dudes who had given me drugs that night, but after he saw my desperation for more, he took me on a car ride just to tell me that I should seriously think about getting help. "I care about you," he said. That felt nice.

I never saw Mason again, but I remember him because he was the first person outside of the alternative program who told me I needed help. That meant more to me than he will ever know.

As I reflect on this time in my life, I can see that my sexual encounters had gotten out of control. But as it was happening, it didn't strike me as a problem. Sex with many partners, just like doing many drugs, seemed normal to me when I looked at Holly and so many other young women and men who were sleeping around. It seemed just as natural as breathing air. Unfortunately, because this was Holly's *and* my norm, she couldn't save me from the life, and I couldn't save her.

Holly and I were the best friends from hell, bent on our mutual destruction. The story that follows perfectly illustrates our union.

One night, I was partying with Holly and some friends, Bonnie and Brad. All four of us were kissing and touching one another in my car, a Chevy Cavalier piece of shit I'd bought for $2,000 with my earnings from cashiering at a clothing store and with help from Mom. I was driving high on acid and ecstasy, snorting cocaine, and smoking pot, drugs I regularly did all together at once at this time in my life. You name it, it was happening in my car. So, of course, I wasn't paying attention to the road.

We approached some train tracks, and suddenly, I heard a very loud horn and saw bright lights. I was too fucked up to realize that the horn and the lights were signaling that a train was barreling down the tracks. I kept driving. I passed the safety guard gate just before it came down, driving over the tracks JUST in time to miss getting smashed by the train—at least that's how I remember it. This was enough to jolt me from my haze. I believe if we had been on those tracks just a few seconds more, I would not be writing this book today. All of our stories would have ended that night. I truly believe that a higher power was looking out for us.

In all these years, I never considered that my luck could one day run out. In that regard, I was a typical teen. I suppose I believed I could do anything and would live forever. But at age seventeen, for the first time I recognized that my actions had consequences and that those consequences could be fatal.

At this age, for the first time I admitted to myself that I was an addict and that this was a bad thing. I had been smoking crystal meth for a week, variously in my Chevy Cavalier, at home when Mom wasn't there, and at friends' houses, when the realization struck. I was sitting in the Cavalier—I don't remember exactly where, maybe a parking lot—as I felt the crystal meth manipulate my system. I looked at myself in my rearview mirror and thought, *I'm never doing this shit again. This is it. I'm done.*

At some point, I passed out in my car. When I awoke, I searched for more shit. I found some pot and got right to it. In that moment, I knew I was using against my will. I had no idea how to stop.

Once I had a substance in my body, all I could think about was how to get more of it. Not everyone who takes drugs feels this compulsion to have more and more. That's the difference between addicts and nonaddicts. Addiction is a scary disease, and only some users have it. My brothers didn't, certainly not Noah. He smoked pot and drank, but he never did hardcore drugs with any regularity.

The fact that Noah was older than Eli and me might be one of the factors that kept him out of the way of hard substances. By the time the drug-crazed rave scene was raging in our 'hood, Noah was out of the house at college. When he would come back to visit and see Eli high on stuff like cocaine, ecstasy, and dust from the raves, he didn't get it. I made sure to hide my use from Noah, so he never saw me. That said, Noah didn't tell Eli to stop using the hardcore stuff, but he didn't join in "the fun" either.

And while Eli's use of hard drugs got out of control, he got off them by his early twenties without any formal intervention program. He never needed to go to detox or rehab.

Despite the fact that sex and drugs fascinated me more than the alternative program, I managed to remain in it all the way through my senior year. That year, I attended it in a middle-class neighborhood in my county.

The program remained easy. I continued to meet the minimum standards of showing up to do the work, being somewhat respectful, and not doing anything too crazy, and at seventeen, I finished the program, which made me a high school graduate. We didn't have a graduation ceremony, so teachers celebrated me and the other students with a classroom party filled with food, games, and laughter.

Then that weekend, about six of us, including a classmate named Drew, pooled our money to rent a limo and buy cocaine and alcohol for a celebratory ride around Long Island. When one of them set the coke in front of me, it was over. I snorted line after line after line until my friends were like, "Yo, Marsha, why don't you just chill out?" I didn't take their advice. I kept using, and my heart started beating really fast.

Soon, the limo dropped us off at Drew's place. There, I ran around his backyard like a lunatic as my heartbeat still raced at Olympic speed. Drew looked at me and said, "I know what will calm you down." He broke out a line and said, "You only need a little bit. Trust me, it's not like coke."

I stared at some light-brown powder. I touched it. It didn't feel like cocaine.

"It's heroin," Drew said.

I snorted it. And just like that, I lost my heroin virginity.

I snorted more. Things started spinning. Soon, I threw off my clothes to reveal my underwear and jumped into Drew's pool—

so my friends told me.

Hours later, when I crept into my house after midnight, my heart was still thumping out of control. I took an over-the-counter sleeping pill to calm down and get some Z's, but it didn't work. I panicked and barged into Eli's room to wake him up. "I think something's wrong," I told him. "I did way too much blow, bro. My heart doesn't feel right."

"Calm down," said Eli. "Try to breathe. You'll be fine in a couple of hours."

He went back to bed, and I went to my room. I lay down staring at the ceiling and praying that I wouldn't have a heart attack.

Later that morning, I woke up feeling like crap. Then I remembered that I had to drive my maternal grandparents, who now lived in the South and had been visiting us for a few days, to the airport. I couldn't wiggle out of it because Eli and Mom had to go to work. All I could think was that my grandparents would take one look at me and figure out that I was on drugs. Sure enough, on the ride to the airport, I began nodding off at the wheel. "You alright, kid?" my grandpa asked. "Yes, I'm just tired," I said, perking back up. He knew I had been out late the night before. I hoped that he bought my excuse.

Throughout all of these years of drugs, sex, and drinking, I don't recall ever once asking Mom for help. I wanted to after crystal meth had kept me up for more than a week, eyes wide open, seeing things, feeling paranoid, heart pounding, having that realization about my addiction in my Cavalier, but I just couldn't bring myself to tell her. Somewhere in my subconscious, I probably thought she would have denied it anyway.

PART TWO

ADDICTION HELL

CHAPTER FIVE

HOPE AND LOSS

As a seventeen-year-old high school graduate, I should have felt like I was moving up in the world. I felt anything but that. My addictions had robbed me of a shot at a four-year college, so instead I blended in with the workforce. I worked as a telemarketer for a mortgage company and a receptionist at a chiropractor's office.

Though I was an addict, I knew how to act "normal" when needed. That's why I got the telemarketer job. During the phone interview, they heard my professional voice, liked my tone, and hired me sight unseen.

As for the chiropractor's office, I had an inside track. My neighbor's daughter was leaving her post there as a receptionist and recommended me for her job. I came in for the interview smartly dressed and acting like a sane job candidate and talked my way into the position. The bosses eventually found out about my substance use. My constant bloodshot eyes and shifting behavior, from warm and fuzzy to avoidant, were clues, but it didn't matter to them. They were a bunch of hippies who did a few drugs themselves. That said, they appreciated the fact that I always showed up for work and performed my job well; but my sometimes strange behavior concerned them and they advised me to seek help. I didn't.

In addition to working, about a year after finishing the alternative program I found time to attend community college, taking sociology, English, and remedial math. I earned a 3.5 grade average, an accomplishment that made me believe, for the first time, that I was smart. But deep down, for me personally, I didn't see the point of traditional academic studies, and by the time I turned nineteen, after only one semester of school, I left the program.

My next stop: I took a modeling and acting class. I had a few artistic dreams. People told me I had a great voice and that I was pretty. I still had doubts about my looks, but I was curious to see if they were right. Maybe I had been too hard on myself. Maybe I *did* have the stuff for Hollywood and magazines. But I would come into class disheveled after a night of clubbing, eyes red with black circles under them, and fall asleep. Despite all of that, the runway coach told me I might have a chance at the modeling game if I got my act together. But I didn't follow his advice, and I left this program too.

One good thing had come from the class though. I met my first *real* boyfriend through one of my classmates. My previous relationships were all fly-by-night. But this guy, Stephen, was the real deal, a keeper.

Stephen was good for me. He wasn't on serious drugs. Yes, he smoked pot, occasionally did nitrous hits—breathing in nitrous oxide from balloons—and drank, but that was nothing like my drug use. He tried to get me off hardcore stuff too. He really cared about me. Additionally, he supported my career aspirations. After I flamed out in the acting and modeling class, I had begun seriously considering a career in massage therapy.

The idea had hatched in my mind at the chiropractor's office, where I was still employed. There, I watched staff work on a few patients and had opportunities to work on some myself. I enjoyed the work. One of the chiropractors had noticed this and suggested that massage therapy might be a good career path for me.

As a kid, I was always touchy-feely. I always felt this ball of energy bouncing around in my hands. And as messed up as I was, I was also a loving kid who wanted to help people, to give them a hug or massage to make them feel good. Regularly, as I rubbed one of my uncle's shoulders and neck, he'd remark on my "impressive strength." Now as an adult, in addition to some of the professionals in the chiropractor's office, this same uncle, and others, including my mom, were encouraging me to go to massage therapy school. Mom told me she had faith that I would succeed in this field, and further, she pledged to pay for all of my schooling.

Mom's reason for pushing me into massage therapy was about more than my strong, nurturing hands. My entire life, I had been highly sensitive to whatever people were feeling. From a very young age, I could tell when something was bothering someone; they didn't have to say anything. I could "feel" when they were in emotional or physical pain. I would look at them, see it in their eyes and their posture, and I would ask them if they were okay. People appreciated my concern. So, from there, they felt comfortable talking to me. And they never heard anything I told them come from someone else's mouth later.

Even the chiropractor's office staff recognized my strong people skills. They saw that others trusted me, and they recognized my empathic nature. So, while I certainly had my problems, I had many gifts as well. I loved to hug people and massage their shoulders. I loved to help people feel better.

After a little research, I applied to a massage therapy school in New Jersey, where Stephen lived, because it was less expensive than schools I had looked into in New York. After the program accepted me, I enrolled in it.

Before I began school, however, Stephen and I got some devastating news from an over-the-counter kit: I was six weeks pregnant.

I sat down next to him on his bed with the test. For a moment, we said nothing. Then Stephen, very calm, began to talk. His stance on the child was clear.

He didn't want it.

He told me that his mother had had him when she was nineteen and that he'd barely had a relationship with his dad.

Stephen and I were both nineteen.

"We don't even have careers or jobs," he said as he hugged me. "We can't do this. This is not an option." He went on, "You're on a lot of drugs. Look at all the drugs you were doing just this summer alone. We were just doing nitrous hits together. Is this child going to be normal? No, we can't do this."

I wasn't convinced. Not long afterward, I called my doctor to find out if the baby had a chance of being normal. I gave him a list of the drugs I was taking. He told me he couldn't give me an answer. I stood at the other end of the phone feeling like I wanted to have the baby, yet I didn't. Then I called Eli. He didn't know what to say, then he asked me if I was sure I really wanted to have a child. I told him no. I was thinking about my plans for massage therapy school and my desire to get my life together. I was crying. I was scared. I wanted to ask Mom what I should do, but I couldn't.

Negative thoughts began to swirl through my head. *I'm not capable of raising a child. The baby could be damaged. I can't stop using.* Stephen knew I wasn't going to stop using too. I was an active drug addict. People loved me and were urging me to stop, but honestly, I could not even go one day without using something and didn't know how to.

Ultimately, I decided that Stephen was right. We couldn't keep the child. We couldn't take the chance.

The week we discovered I was pregnant, I made an appointment to see a doctor.

Stephen entered a clinic room with me. As I lay on an examination table, I looked at a monitor showing our baby. For a split second, I looked away. I didn't want to go through with the abortion . . . but minutes later, I let a nurse escort me into another room, where I let someone give me anesthesia . . . and sometime later, I woke up no longer a mother.

Afterward, Stephen drove me home, and he, Eli, and I hung out at Mom's house. She wasn't there. We smoked joints in the kitchen.

I smoked to block out what had just happened. Eventually, we made it to the living room couch, where I fell asleep on Stephen's lap.

What I did that day was the culmination of the toughest decision of my entire life. Afterward, I decided that something good had to come from it. I was going to go to massage therapy school and become a success.

A few weeks later, I moved to Jersey for school and began working in a coffee shop. One of the waitresses, all of twenty-two years old, told me that she had a three-year-old son. She had given birth to him when she was nineteen. I stood there and thought, *She decided to have her kid and I didn't.* That shook me. I couldn't stand where my feet were placed. I excused myself for the restroom and cried in a stall.

I thought I knew in my heart that I had done the right thing, but at the same time, I questioned whether I really had. I knew addicts who had given birth to children with physical and emotional problems and some whose children had come out totally healthy. Maybe my child would have been healthy. I'll never know.

I cried a lot before and after the abortion. My choice fucked me up, and honestly, it still fucks me up. After the abortion, I promised myself that if I ever became pregnant again, I would have the child.

But as of this writing, I have yet to conceive again. I have tried many times.

Though I struggled with the decision I made about my child, I knew that I had to maintain a forward-looking mindset in order to succeed in massage therapy school—so I tried to remain focused on the future and stay positive.

Good thing I did that. I discovered that the program was everything I had hoped it would be and more.

My studies underscored that I was called to work on people with my hands. Furthermore, I excelled in the program because, as it turns out, I am a visual and tactile learner, something I hadn't understood until my massage studies began. It was one thing to read about subjects, but as I worked with plastic "skeletons" and watched videos that featured cadavers, my understanding of massage took off.

In addition to this, I listened to tapes repeatedly and used flash cards to memorize concepts. These study methods, which I devised on my own, helped me better focus my attention.

As a younger person struggling with learning disabilities all those years ago, maybe I would have achieved a better educational outcome had my teachers and I understood that I needed to see and touch lessons to effectively learn. But now, with this new understanding about myself, for the first time in my academic life, I was concentrating. I was learning! I was loving it. I was becoming a master of the art of massage.

Many people don't understand just how much you need to know about the human body to earn a certification as a massage therapist, and I didn't either until I became a student in the program. It broke down our studies into Western and Eastern theories. Among the Western topics: anatomy, the study of the structure of the body, and physiology, the study of how all the parts of the body make it work. Western studies taught me how to help people relax, relieve their tension, improve their circulation and flexibility, and manage their chronic pain.

As for Eastern practices, they involve healing based on energy flow and attaining positive energy in the human mind and form. The massage that results helps rid people of negative toxins and brings in positive blood flow. The theory from the East espouses that every part of the body has points leading to different organs and that certain types of massages, such as shiatsu and Thai massage, open up these pathways to bring healing to the body, mind, and soul.

In addition to the Eastern and Western theories, I learned all different types of massage techniques, including Swedish massage, therapeutic massage, deep tissue massage, neuromuscular therapy, prenatal massage, hot stone massage, and sports massage.

The program taught me how to work on people of all different shapes and sizes as well as people with injuries, herniated or bulging discs, moles, diseases such as the human immunodeficiency virus (HIV), cancer, and Parkinson's, as well as burn victims, diabetics, and those suffering from multiple sclerosis. I learned how to work on abuse victims who might exhibit strong emotional responses on the massage table, such as crying, too.

Over the course of the year, I was really digging my studies, especially when I applied them on real people. In practice sessions, I discovered that I became more curious about their lives the more I got to know them. If they wanted to share their stories with me, I wanted to hear them.

My studies built upon my natural skills for reading people, and that skill set expanded. Now, just by looking at someone's posture, I could tell if one hip or shoulder was higher than the other, for instance, or if the person had lower back, neck, knee, or ankle issues. By watching how a person walked, held a body part, or if they rubbed their neck or head, squinted, or were hunched over, I knew if they had a headache or what other part of their body hurt.

How I read people and my love for healing translated into how I massaged them on the table. Soon, instructors were telling me that I was a natural massage therapist, strong, and that a wonderful energy flowed from me to the people I worked on.

Their praise meant a great deal to me. Their encouraging words about my gift for healing and their genuine interest in my success put me on a natural high and inspired me to keep on. So, while some other students dropped out over the course of the program, about a year after my enrollment, I graduated with a 93 average.

Mom radiated pride. I stood on the cusp of doing what she had taught me: to support myself and stand on my own feet. To celebrate that, she surprised me with a trip to Italy.

We visited the island of Capri, where we marveled over the gorgeous blue-green water. We visited Rome, where we oohed and aahed on our tour of the Vatican and the Sistine Chapel. I'll never forget a painting of Jesus from which his eyes seemed to follow us wherever we walked. Talk about trippy! We visited the site of Julius Caesar's assassination as well as St. Peter's Square, the large plaza in front of St. Peter's Basilica, and the Colosseum, the large amphitheater with the partially destroyed outer wall.

The site of Pompeii affected me the most. Standing in the midst of the ruins and ashes of the most famous and tragic volcanic eruption left me speechless. To think that this tragedy happened in 79 AD, yet when we stood in that sacred space, I could feel the spirits of the dead nearly 2,000 years later. I knew that I would always treasure this experience I shared with Mom.

Joy filled Mom because I had figured out what I wanted to do with my life.

Joy filled me too. I felt thankful for the trip, grateful. I felt proud of myself, accomplished.

Meanwhile, throughout our time in Italy, Mom never pried into my personal life or hinted that she might know I had an addiction. However, wine sat on restaurant tables morning, noon, and night, and I drank. Mom made a point of telling me, "Mush, just because the wine is on the table at every meal doesn't mean you have to drink it." I told her, "What do you mean? It's here, so of course we do!"

With that, Mom said nothing more about the subject.

CHAPTER SIX

A DEEP SPIRAL

Shortly after I finished massage therapy school, I moved back into my childhood home on Long Island to establish my career. I did so because I didn't like the idea of Mom living alone. Even though I had wanted more from her over the years, to put it plainly, I still loved her.

On the wings of that love, I wanted to do right by Mom's investment in my future; she had kept her word and paid for every stitch of my massage therapy studies. So, I wanted to show her that I could live up to my potential to become a great massage therapist. But quickly after returning home, I found myself doing hardcore drugs in a big way again, something I had largely given up while attending school and living with Stephen. He had been okay with me smoking pot and drinking, but he had helped me mostly stay off the hard stuff by not allowing it into his apartment.

However, after finding employment as a massage therapist for a day spa in Long Island's affluent Nassau County, I tripped up because the atmosphere was rife with coke. The hairstylists snorted it on the job, so I figured, what the hell, if they could do drugs on the job, so could I, and so I did. Then after work, I'd hang out at bars with some of them and we'd head to a restroom stall to do more blow.

When Stephen realized that I was back to my old ways, he gave me an ultimatum: him or coke. I chose coke. I loved Stephen, but often, when I thought about how he had urged me to get the abortion, I resented him too. Now, drugs gave me an excuse to end things with him, to remove from my life the man who was a daily reminder of the child I would never know.

My job at the Nassau County spa only lasted a few months because I found better-paying work at a day spa in my home county of Suffolk. On a good day there, I was making about $500. This was dangerous money, because I couldn't resist using it to buy more drugs.

After work, I'd switch out of my plain black pants, top, and sneakers and into my combat boots, tight jeans, and T-shirt, and, with my rainbow-colored hair—I was a product of the grunge era after all—I'd leave the spa for the strip club where Holly was performing. After graduation, she'd found her way to fast money through erotic dancing, and she thought I should get involved. She and her friends were always trying to get me to dance, but I just couldn't take my clothes off for money. *I just couldn't do it!* But I'd sure spend my cash on coke at the club and make out with girls.

During this time, I also dated a guy I'll call Brian, a good friend of Eli's. This relationship sent me further down the addiction hole. Brian was the first full-blown crackhead I ever knew and the first person I was aware of who would do almost anything for drugs. He stole valuables from his family's house and took them to the pawn shop to pay for his habit. His dad made trips to retrieve the stuff from the store all of the time. I didn't find out all of this until I got involved with Brian.

Quickly, Brian's lifestyle began to affect me. I started smoking crack on the regular, something I'd only done a few times before. Once you do that stuff seriously, it's hard to stop. All drugs are evil, but that one, to me, is one of the most evil of all. As soon as I'd take a twenty-dollar hit, I needed another one. That drug would literally have me up for days at a stretch until I would pass out trying to figure out ways to get more. And it was easy to get; after all, the police had once called New York the world's "crack capital," and though crack use was now on the decline in the city, plenty of dealers were still happy to sell it.

In the midst of this drama-filled time at the start of my career, I managed to take private classes with a Reiki Master. I had massaged her at the Suffolk County spa a few times before she urged me to study under her. "You have so much talent in your hands," she told me. "You have so much potential to take this to a whole other level."

Reiki is the Japanese practice of laying hands to bring healing. It accomplishes this by drawing out negative energy and clearing a person's aura, their energy field, and chakras, their physical and spiritual energy, to bring in positive energy. My Reiki Master would watch me practice the craft in her home studio and praise my work. She also knew I had a drug problem. My boss, who had figured out I was a drug user after I'd come to work high one time too many, had told her. One day, the Reiki Master cornered me about it. "You're throwing away your potential," she told me. "You have a natural gift, and if you would get clean, your career possibilities could be endless."

I could hear what she was saying, but I couldn't comprehend it.

In addition to her, others were urging me to get help as well. My boss happened to be engaged to a man who had been clean for fifteen years after a battle with active drug addiction. He knew I had come to work high and had asked my boss to give me more chances. He was always encouraging me to come with him to one of his twelve-step meetings too.

The first time he mentioned twelve steps, I didn't have a clue what he was talking about. I didn't know such programs existed, and if it had been mentioned in the alternative program, I hadn't been listening. I didn't realize that people met in groups to discuss their drug use to stop using drugs altogether. Ultimately, I didn't go to a meeting with my boss's fiancé, but it was nice to know someone cared.

The fiancé and my Reiki Master were right, however. I really needed to get help. I had dabbled in crack and heroin off and on, but now I was doing them all the time, mixing them together in what's called a speedball, and this was eating into my wallet at a clip of easily $300 a day. The drug use was affecting my career too. The drugs made me ill, so I couldn't always work.

Enter Gabe, a friend I made through another massage therapist at my Suffolk County boss's other spa, on Suffolk's Fire Island, where I had begun to work as well. Gabe, a drug addict and alcoholic, knew about my drug use and that I also drank. He insisted on taking me to my first meeting for addicts, a group for alcoholics that he frequented.

At the meeting, I told a few people that I didn't have a drinking problem but that I did a few drugs. They told me that I didn't belong with them and that I needed to meet with other drug addicts. That made me angry, so I left the room, with Gabe not too far behind me. *How dare they say I'm a drug addict!* I thought. Deep inside, I rejoiced over the fact that they said I didn't belong because that gave me an excuse to leave. I never went back.

The great thing about that one encounter, however, is that the stories the men and women told about wanting to get better showed me that I didn't want to stay with Brian. My gut was telling me that he would ruin my life. To top things off, Brian had stolen jewelry and a gold coin from me to pay for drugs, just like he'd robbed his own family. After reflecting on all of this, I broke up with him.

Writing about Brian robbing people to buy drugs brings up a memory that makes me look like a hypocrite because it involves me robbing people too. Once, Holly and I stole cocaine from her drug-dealing boyfriend. After he found out, he pointed a gun at our heads and said he'd kill us if we ever did it again. Do you know what? He didn't scare me. I just looked at him, probably with a sneer, and thought, *Dude, really?* I had a fuck-you attitude when instead I should have been praying for my life. But that's what being high does to you—it takes you out of your right mind. A few years later, this man would no longer prove a threat to Holly and me or anyone else. He was found dead from suicide.

Holly and the strip club scene would put me in the path of other negative experiences, like Logan. The first time I saw him, he was spinning records at the club. This guy was a really great DJ and hot to boot, nearly six feet tall, with a medium build and short blond hair.

Logan looked real good to me after dealing with Brian.

I thought things could only improve.

Wrong!

Logan had had a falling out with his father and had nowhere to go, so not long after we began dating, he wound up living with me at Mom's. Mom had bought his story that he needed a place to lay his head. She thought she was helping him, but in hindsight, I see that this was part of her enabling behavior.

Quickly, Logan began disrupting our lives. He was only supposed to stay for a few days, but a few days became a few weeks, then more than a month. He wouldn't leave our house, though we asked him to. Finally, I couldn't let him stay there while I was gone and my mother was at work, so I'd take him with me to my spa job on Fire Island, where I was now working exclusively. As I worked, he'd rollerblade for hours. He was thirty years old.

All of Logan's shenanigans began to weigh on me, and I couldn't focus on the job. The stress caused me to use even more drugs.

My boss noticed that my performance was getting worse, and since I'd brought Logan to work with me a time too many, she had an inkling that he was exacerbating my drug problem. She urged me to break up with him. I did.

This breakup turned very ugly.

After I sent Logan packing, he became crazy and started to stalk me. He moved into a rental almost right around the corner from my house and began to harass me. No exaggeration, he called me 100 to 150 times a day on my cell phone. He came to my house at three a.m. banging down my door once, and all my mom could say was, "Marsha, are you gonna do something about this?" Meanwhile, my boss was urging me to get a restraining order against him.

Again, I followed her advice.

I wanted Mom by my side when I applied for the order, but she said she couldn't go with me because she had to work. At this point, Eli had moved to Denver, Colorado, to live with Noah, who was now a restaurant manager. With my brothers so far away, I couldn't call on them. And my friends were drug addicts. They couldn't help themselves let alone me.

It took two restraining orders to convince Logan to give up the harassing phone calls and visits. But when someone has stalked you, it can remain a messy problem for years. Logan would continue to follow me like a shadow. A few years after the second restraining order, he called me to make amends. I thanked him, but that phone call led to more and more calls. So, I called the cops, who turned around and confronted Logan, telling him to leave me alone or else.

You would think that the drama with Logan would have opened Mom's eyes to my problems, but it didn't. I believe that she wanted everything to be perfect and didn't want to see that things were far from that. But my time with my next boyfriend, Cole, would finally shatter her innocence and force her to accept the truth.

I was a semifunctional addict, more or less newly broken up with Logan, when I met this guy Cole on Long Island. I was smoking crack big time while barely maintaining my job and some semblance of a life.

Cole had been clean for a few years before we got together. I inspired his relapse.

After he took me out for the first time, on a dinner date, we came back to my house. Mom was not home, so I got high in front of Cole. I pretty much blew crack smoke in his face, and he was like, "Okay, little girl, you want to know how to smoke crack? I will show you what crack is about." True to his word, Cole, who was ten years older than me, educated me about the world of crack, and over the course of his tutorial, we became crack-smoking equals. We smoked tons of it and constantly looked for more. Between the two of us, we often shelled out $500 a day for the drug and sometimes as much as a grand. We did lots of heroin too.

My increased drug use became extremely apparent at work, too much for my boss to ignore. One day, she had it with me coming in sick and finally told me what she had bottled up for months. "You have a natural ability that took me years of schooling to get, and you're throwing it away." I blew off her words like they meant nothing. She fired me.

My disease had so entangled me that I could embrace nothing but it. In the back of my mind, I knew that I could read people and help them, but I just didn't care.

I was twenty-one and going nowhere but down.

My life spiraled out of control while I dated Cole. He had lots of time and some money on his hands to get in trouble. He'd been laid off from his job, which I won't identify, and he was throwing his unemployment checks away on drugs.

While I smoked crack with Cole, I was out of work for more than a year. My "large" body, always the bane of my existence, whittled down to a size two from about a size six. My clothes hung off me. My skin appeared gray, and my shoulder bones stuck out. Black circles ringed my eyes.

I was now a full-blown drug addict.

With Cole, I went on a drug run of a lifetime, a rampage. We traveled all over New York City to get ourselves into some shit to get high. We liked to get our drugs there because they were still generally cheaper in the city than on Long Island, so we could get more for less, though we still paid a fortune. We robbed people. I stole credit cards from friend's handbags and Cole stole money from his family to pay for our $500-a-day habit. Dealers robbed us too, by selling us fake drugs.

Cole got his ass kicked and his nose broken so many times in scuffles. From Harlem to Washington Heights, my father's old neighborhood as a youth, we hung out in hot-as-hell crack houses with no electricity in the summer and with reeking shit in the corners. In the 1980s, Washington Heights was known as *the* place in all of America to get crack because so much was sold there, and let me tell you, there was still a lot of it to be had in that neighborhood when Cole and I frequented it in the early 2000s.

Once, I disappeared from one of the crack houses Cole and I were in, and he thought some dude had kidnapped me. I was just out getting high with the guy. No problems.

In general, I was popular with all of the guys. In particular, the black men on the streets had a nickname for me; they called me "90210," a reference to the hit '90s show *Beverly Hills, 90210* about a bunch of rich white kids. They said the name fit me because I was a pretty white girl who always had money and wouldn't sell her ass for crack. "Keep smoking this shit, 90210," they told me, "and one day we will have you." I told them I would rob my mother before I'd fuck anyone for money, and so I did. I stole her credit cards, her cash, her jewelry, her rest.

I stole the money right from Mom's purse, which she kept on the kitchen table. With it, I'd take these drug dealers shopping to buy them sneakers, clothes, TVs, appliances, PlayStations, DVD players, baby food, diapers, you name it, in exchange for drugs. I rang up thousands of dollars between a bunch of my credit cards and, eventually, something like $7,000 on one of Mom's cards, which took her a minute to realize before she canceled it and ultimately confronted me about using drugs . . . but I'm getting ahead of the story.

To stay high, I did some other really bad shit. I used to rob Home Depot and repeatedly return the stuff to get money. Eventually, employees blacklisted me from making returns. Another crazy thing I did: I rented out my truck, a Dodge Durango, for a few hits of crack. Once, my crack dealer returned it with the driver's side all scratched and crashed up. Honestly, I couldn't say shit. What was I going to do? Call my insurance company and tell them my dealer fucked my truck up? Oh wait, I didn't have insurance!

The Durango. That brings up other memories. That's the car Cole and I drove to hit one place after another after I lost my driver's license after cops pulled me over for driving with no car insurance and registration. And in Cole's car, a Chevy Blazer truck with essentially no working brakes—we always used the emergency brakes—we drove around with two different plates that we stole off other cars. At this point, I had a dog, Heidi, a mini-dachshund, who had liver disease. When she wasn't at home with Mom, I took her with me on some of these runs. Shameful.

As you can see, I sunk to some real lows for drugs, but I never prostituted and NO that definitely doesn't make me better than anyone who did, and I'll tell you why . . .

Right after I broke up with Stephen, I hooked up with dealers who used to be my childhood friends just to get free drugs. I never thought of that as prostitution, because technically it wasn't. But that's the point: It was a technicality. I now understand that though I didn't trade sex for money, I still used my body to get what I wanted, just like a prostitute does. Honestly, I was mostly a tease and didn't sleep with everyone and still got free drugs.

I used dudes that I called my friends, or called suckers, for their drugs. I hooked up with a hot-looking dealer who was black, Italian, and Spanish to get free coke from him all the time. I got high with prostitutes, some of whom were pregnant, too. But I never wanted to be that girl who turned a trick on the street for the next one, and the prostitutes I used drugs with in crack motels didn't want me to be that girl either.

While I never "officially prostituted," it crossed my mind as a possibility a few times when I dated Cole. The fact is, I wasn't thinking about much else except how I could get "the next one." I was so young, so skinny, so desperate, so disappeared. I disappeared for weeks at a time to binge on drugs. Once, after I disappeared into a crack house with Cole for nearly a week, we had lots of sex and literally passed out for two days in his studio apartment in Nassau County. I woke up with a crack pipe in my mouth and immediately took a hit. Then I felt a ringing in my ears and lightheaded, euphoric. Cole started taking the hits too, and we kept taking them until we passed out again.

During this crazy time, my mother worried herself sick not knowing if I was dead or alive. I'd call her once a week or pop into the house saying I was going to get a pack of cigarettes, and then I'd disappear. After a week of hanging out in Cole's apartment, and sometimes after being up for more or less five days straight because I couldn't fall asleep, I'd come home filthy dirty because I hadn't showered in days. I'd time my trips home to coincide with Mom being at work or when I figured she was at what was now her steady boyfriend's house. I'd only stay overnight when I was aiming to steal from her purse. During this time, Mom thought I was living with Cole. She didn't even know that I had lost my job.

I didn't always get the timing right in my attempts to avoid Mom. I ran into her a few times smelling bad, looking bad, acting extremely strange, even for me. And for the first time, my behavior seemed to be catching her attention. Between her missing cash and rung-up credit cards and my poor hygiene, she knew something was wrong and began demanding answers. Of course, I told her that she was exaggerating and that everything was okay. She didn't accuse me of using drugs, but she insisted that I wasn't telling the truth about being okay. Then one day she threatened to take away Heidi and get my brothers involved if that's what she needed to do to help me.

My behavior wore Mom down. Some nights when I was home, I heard her crying in her bedroom. I tortured her soul and her emotions. I took away her sleep. I made her life unmanageable. It hurt me to see her like this, but I didn't know how to change my actions. So, finally, Mom followed through on her threat to bring in Eli and Noah. They flew from Denver to spend time with me in our childhood home. But when they arrived, I was on another run with Cole. Several days later, when I returned, my brothers looked at me with complete and utter sadness, disappointment, and fear.

They urged me to go back to Denver with them to get clean, and so I did—go to Denver that is. Now mind you, they smoked pot and drank, but Eli had given up the hard stuff, like I told you, and Noah had never really done it. Meanwhile, neither of them saw anything wrong with me smoking pot, but they wanted me to stay away from crack and drugs of that caliber. The thing is, to get clean, someone like me shouldn't have been doing *any* drugs. Any drug I did made me want more. My brothers didn't understand that.

So guess what? I smoked pot with them. Then when they were at work, I wound up having sex with one of their male friends. Next thing you know, this guy and I snorted cocaine and then visited a strip club, where I hooked up with a couple of hot strippers. Talk about an intervention that turned into an epic failure.

So back at home, I went back to Cole.

I had to become a total crackhead, shooting up coke and heroin and robbing and stealing from Mom for her to finally see, or perhaps I should say "accept," that I was in trouble. But it took her sister Janet visiting our home after a death in the family to force Mom to take serious corrective action with me.

It happened after I gave Aunt Janet a shocking fright-sight: She found me passed out in my bed after another run with Cole. I opened my eyes to find her rubbing my head as tears ran down her face. Then she ran downstairs yelling at my mother, saying in her characteristic plainspoken way, "If you don't start doing something about your daughter, you're going to have one dead daughter on your hands."

She continued, shouting, "She's so skinny. She's gray. Fucking open your eyes. What the fuck is the matter with you? She's really sick, and she needs help. She needs you to help her do something, or she's going to die and you have to live with that for the rest of your life. You're not helping her. You're enabling her. You need to force her into detox and rehab or do something. Now go upstairs and break through the denial." I'm paraphrasing all of this, of course, but that's what I remember my aunt essentially saying.

After this incident, Mom began growing a pair of balls. She had always wanted to be there for me—that's why she had never kicked me out of the house—but she just didn't know how to help. Later, she would tell me that she really hadn't understood just how bad my condition was, even after getting Noah and Eli involved. After my trip to Denver, my brothers had probably covered for me like they had my whole life and probably hadn't revealed to Mom the extent of my problem.

Now, at Aunt Janet's urging, Mom began to demand that I go into detox and rehab. It would be a few years before I would actually get clean and stay clean, but thank God, the push I needed had finally arrived.

Of course, I wasn't thanking God at the time. If anything, I was angry as the devil.

Not feeling one iota like going to a detox center and a rehab facility, I called my friend Gabe, the guy who had taken me to that meeting for alcoholics that one time. I needed his advice. Gabe had been in detox and rehab and knew the score. He talked to me about it and offered to drive me to a crisis center. He picked me up from my house and off we went. My mother had met Gabe before. She trusted him and was grateful for his help.

Gabe and I shared a unique relationship. After Logan, and before my relationship with Cole became serious, I had slept with Gabe briefly, and in those times, Gabe had refused to get high with me. He was a thirtysomething guy who had been in and out of prison for drug-related crimes for many years and didn't want me to suffer the same fate. Now, he was on a mission to help me. I can still hear him saying, "Marsha, you do not want to end up like me. Get your shit together because you will end up a junkie on the street selling your ass one day. You will end up in jail too, or dead. If you don't think that's true, keep doing this shit and watch your yets become agains."

He was right. Poor Gabe. He couldn't get his shit together for longer than six months at a clip, but he lifted me up at one of the lowest points in my life. Later, he wound up going back to prison for ten years because of a drug-related crime. I wrote to him, but when he got out, we lost touch. I have no idea where he is now.

But when I was twenty-two, Gabe was very much present in my life. With his help, I registered at a crisis center on Long Island to detox. My mom's health insurance, which still covered me, would largely pay for my stay there and at subsequent centers.

At the first detox ward, I stayed for twelve days. In that time, my assigned counselor put me through a psychological evaluation and asked me to reveal all the drugs I was using. When I completed reciting the list, he looked at me and actually said, "Are you serious? Are you exaggerating?"

I asked him if I looked like I was exaggerating. In response, he told me I was lucky to be alive. I blew off the whole conversation like it wasn't a big deal.

After the twelve days of detoxing, a van picked me up to take me to a twenty-eight-day rehab program on Long Island. I didn't last there long. On day three, I packed up my few things and walked right out of the facility and down the road to a police station. I made up some story and somehow convinced a cop to drive me home.

You have to remember, when I walked into the detox facility and the rehab center, I still wasn't willing to get clean. I was a crackhead on the street. I was the person who would scream at the birds in the morning to "Shut the fuck up!" because it sounded like they were coming for me. Hell, I probably would have shot them if I'd had a gun. Remember, I was robbing my mother to pay for drugs. Honestly, I would have robbed your mother for the next one. I had rented my truck out to get high. I had stolen steaks, diapers, and baby formula from stores to sell them on the street to get the next one with Cole.

I just wasn't ready.

After the cop dropped me off at home, I tried my key in the locks and couldn't get in. Mom had changed them. Then I walked over to a neighbor's house, where I called Cole to ask for a ride.

He picked me up but made it clear that he didn't want to get high with me. He told me to get my life together. But I wasn't ready to do that, and I made that clear to him.

So, with neither of us ready to get clean, off we went, back to our runs.

Cole and I continued to hang out in abandoned buildings, in our trucks, and on corners waiting for dealers. We panhandled all over Long Island and New York City. I'm talking about true desperation. I was a mess and hated myself. After completing one of our runs, a car almost hit me. Cole and I had been up for days. We were standing in the middle of morning rush-hour traffic in Manhattan. I was in a mental fog.

Somehow, Cole managed to make it across the street, but I was still stuck in traffic. Drivers were honking their horns as I made a mad dash across the road, jumping over a divider. The cars missed me by seconds. I made it to the other side. I laughed as if I liked the rush of almost losing my life. Did I have no concept of my own life? Did I not care? Or had the drugs taken over to the point where nothing mattered anymore—not my life, my health, my family, and friends? I didn't have money or a job. I was tired of getting sick, but I still wasn't done. I still wasn't ready to surrender.

By this point, I had figured out the code to unlock the garage door at home, so after this run, I crept back into my house and managed to make it upstairs and into the shower. As the water rained on me, I cried hysterically. When I emerged from the bathroom, Mom stood right outside the door. She embraced me, and I cried in her arms and told her I couldn't stop and that I didn't know why, but that I didn't want to do this anymore. For two days, I passed out at home. But let me tell you something: When I came to, ate, and took another shower, I left the house and did the same fucking thing again. It was pure insanity, doing the same thing over and over and expecting a different result.

While I was doing the same thing repeatedly, Mom had left her old ways behind. The easygoing mother that I had known no longer existed. She was taking responsibility for me *and* herself. For one, she had attended a meeting for parents of addicts, where she encountered people who were just like her, people who had lived in denial about their children's drug problem. In the meeting, other parents had told her that she was the problem, that she had enabled me. She didn't want to hear these things, but for the first time, she *was* listening.

Another sign of her 180-degree turnaround: After crying hysterically in the shower after that death-defying run with Cole, Mom began to demand that I go to another detox program. During this time, she was making me see a psychologist too. I'd nod off in session, and he'd tell me he couldn't help me if I was asleep, so he refused to see me again until I got clean.

Meanwhile, I entered detox for a second time just to shut Mom up, and she made it clear that Heidi would not be waiting for me when I got out. Heidi required special care because of her liver disease—care that I was not equipped to give.

After five days of detoxing, staff released me and I repeatedly called Cole, hoping to get high with him, but he didn't answer. Finally, I called this guy Todd, who had given me his number when we met at my very first detox center, and he answered right away. We met up, shot up heroin, and I had sex with him because I was angry at Cole for not answering his phone. I also did it because I felt I needed to have sex with Todd because he'd given me free drugs. Stupid thinking.

Even more stupid, I turned around and told Cole that I had cheated on him. He hated me. Why did I tell him? Maybe subconsciously I just wanted the run and our relationship to end. I was so damn tired, and I knew if I stayed with him, I would never stop the chase.

Though I had cheated on and hurt Cole, however, we got back together and went on another coke-shooting, heroin-crazed run. We fueled it with cash and what remained of Cole's unemployment checks, but finally we simply ran out of money. That left Cole and me desperate for drugs to get that next high. So, we brainstormed how to make that happen. We started talking about the possibility of me prostituting myself for cash. As we spoke, I sat in Cole's truck not even believing what was coming out of my mouth. *Prostitution?*

I broke.

"Cole, I can't live like this anymore," I said.

Cole looked into my eyes. He agreed with me. He didn't want me selling myself on the streets either. We put the notion of prostitution off the table.

Instead, with a new house key Mom had given me, I returned home and stole money from her. She had started sleeping with her purse by her side, but my robbery skills were excellent. I managed to take her money without waking her. Cole and I then went out and got and did more drugs for a few days.

This would be my last run with Cole. The fact that we had seriously considered prostitution had overwhelmed me.

I told Cole that I just couldn't stay in the relationship. The sentiment was mutual, and we ended things. Believe it or not, Cole wanted me to get better. He thought our breakup might help me get off drugs. It may sound crazy to an outsider, but we did care about each other in our own way.

Not long after my relationship with Cole ended, Mom forced me to enter another detox program, my third one, and a rehab center, my second one, in upstate New York.

I went, and though I had broken up with Cole to get better, I was still not ready to give up drugs or the lifestyle that comes with them.

In my early twenties, I was so wrapped up in my disease of addiction that I could not see beyond it. I knew that I had a gift for healing people because that's what everyone was telling me, but I was not embracing that gift or caring about it.

The woman with the healing hands could not heal herself.

CHAPTER SEVEN

REHAB RECAP

I've been in and out of rehab and related programs enough times that often when I tell others about these experiences, the order and number of times confuses them. So, I hope this chapter clears up any questions. Here's my recap:

I detoxed and entered a rehab program the first time at age twenty-two. I stayed at the detox facility, a crisis center on Long Island, for twelve days, observed by staff as I came down from the effects of drugs without the help of any medication. Then staff transferred me by vehicle to a state-run rehab facility, also on Long Island, where I stayed for three days, not completing the program.

About a month after returning from my first detox and rehab experience, Mom made me undergo detox for a second time, this time at a hospital, and she took Heidi away, telling me I would not get her back until I was clean. At the hospital, I detoxed for five days under medical supervision. Staff gave me the synthetic narcotic methadone, used to wean addicts off heroin. When I got out of the hospital, I used drugs again almost immediately probably because I did not go to a rehab center afterward.

A few months after my second detox experience, I entered a third detox program and my second rehab program, which I'll call Gracia Detox and Benevolence Manor, respectively, both in upstate New York. This occurred shortly after Cole and I broke up. I detoxed at Gracia for five days, again on methadone, before arriving at Benevolence, where I stayed for twenty-eight days of rehab. Afterward, I came back to Long Island, where I visited an outpatient facility to get drug tested once a week, one of Mom's stipulations for me coming home. I also began group therapy and counseling on Long Island in a twelve-step program for the first time ever.

The twelve-step program suggested that I attend ninety step meetings in ninety days, get a sponsor, someone who had been clean for a minimum of one year and could mentor me on a journey through the steps, and become involved in a step group close to home. I got a sponsor, but I was not ready to commit to going to all the meetings and hanging out regularly with a group. But I did start making friends in the program, occasionally meeting with people to talk about my experiences, share coffee, and get to know them. This support helped me stay off drugs for fifty-eight days, a personal record.

During this time, I begged, cried, and pleaded to get Heidi back. Mom saw that I was trying to get my life together and thought I would give Heidi the care that her medical condition required, so she gave me Heidi. She shouldn't have.

I was not ready to get clean. After day fifty-eight of no drugs and alcohol, I hooked up with a guy I'd met in a step meeting and shot up heroin with him for two weeks. You see, you can find whatever you want in recovery. If you get clean and stay clean, you can get with people who are recovering from this thing; but if you want to get laid or find someone to do drugs with, surely you can find that in the meetings too. We all know which one I chose in the beginning. So, I failed to stay clean because I had not gotten honest with myself. My issues went beyond drugs, but I hadn't faced that yet.

This is a good point to pause before I wrap up my blow-by-blow by-the-numbers account of my rehab stays to give you a sense of what happened in rehab.

Rehab was always a bonding experience. People talked about their deep feelings and emotions in groups, one time coed, the other times same sex.

My first rehab experience at the center on Long Island was coed. Men and women sat together under a gazebo and told war stories about their active addiction. We learned that some of us had been court mandated to attend rehab while others were there because their wives, husbands, or significant others had threatened to leave them if they didn't get treatment. Some didn't have anywhere else to go or their children had been taken away from them or they were just sick and tired and desperate. We'd talk about how to stay clean, what our addiction triggers were, and what we thought we would do when we got out of rehab and went about life without using drugs.

In my second rehab experience at Benevolence Manor, I attended an all-women's group. The men were kept on the other side of the building, and we were not allowed contact with them. But whether coed or same sex, we talked about largely the same things, though in the women's group we shared more with one another about relationships, sexual abuse issues, and things that we might have done or that had happened to us that we didn't feel comfortable sharing with guys. Just like in the coed group, however, we laughed a lot and made fun of one another.

We had to laugh because if we didn't, we'd be forced to face the destruction we had wrought in so many people's lives, including our own. When we talked, we'd leave out the parts about how we had hurt so many people because mentioning that could stir up feelings of guilt and shame, which could make us want to get high again to numb those feelings.

Another distinction of the all-women's group: Some of us met informally, specifically late at night. When we couldn't sleep, we'd sit around the cafeteria to talk, laugh, play games, and pig out on hot chocolate and graham crackers with peanut butter. You always knew who the heroin addicts were because we were the ones who could never sleep.

At the end of the day, each rehab facility had three main things in common: One, the twentysomething participants talked about their parents a lot. As we did, we learned that most of our parents were enablers who had turned a blind eye to our drug use or had severely underestimated it. They didn't want to believe that we were on drugs, or, on the flip side, they themselves were on drugs or were in jail because of drugs. Most parents had admitted to themselves that we were addicts only after we had stolen from them numerous times, disappeared for weeks, or overdosed. Only then, usually years later, did they snap the fuck out of their denial because they had no choice. They had preferred to look at life through rose-colored glasses because that protective shade had prevented them from looking at themselves and admitting that maybe they had made a mistake, maybe they could have done better by us.

The other two things the facilities had in common: We heard from guest speakers in recovery who shared their success stories about getting clean and how great life could be off drugs. And we learned that some people were in rehab for other people while others were there for themselves.

At this time, I fell into the former group: I was in rehab for other people.

Back to my relapse after fifty-eight days clean: This relapse lasted only two weeks because a surprising sense of self-anger, a first for me, motivated me to give the clean lifestyle another try. Something miraculous was happening. Despite having fought the rehab efforts, somehow "the message of hope and the promise of freedom" that the centers espoused were seeping into my thick head. Somehow, the idea that I might one day recover from my disease had been born inside me.

Once, I had told Cole I loved him, and he had laughed at me and said, "You don't love me, and I don't love you." He told me, "You don't even love your dog" as he smashed the walls of a motel with a hammer, which he typically kept in his truck along with other tools. He was enraged because he thought an older dude who had been in the room with us had stolen his crack pipe. "You have no idea what love is," he continued. "You know what you love?" He then took a hit and a shot of cocaine and said, "Here, Marsha. This is what you fucking love, and this is what I fucking love. People who love each other don't do this shit." I cried and screamed because I knew deep down he was right. I didn't care about a thing except getting the next one.

The new emerging me reflected on my old boyfriend's words and knew that I did not want to be that person anymore. So, I committed myself to a step group, kept in regular touch with my sponsor, and made more step meetings. My commitment to changing my life would lead to my longest stretch clean in what was now my nearly twenty-three years on this earth: thirteen months.

CHAPTER EIGHT

BREAKING POINT

During my thirteen months off drugs, I was getting my life back. I had a job with two spas on Long Island, and I made house calls. My family started trusting me again. The forgiveness of others was helping me stay on the right track.

One of my two jobs, in a spa at a gym, came by way of a new business owner, Teri, whom I had massaged in the Fire Island spa. She knew my story. Teri had used her power as a new spa owner to take a chance on me. I was grateful and thanked her profusely for the opportunity.

I did a good job for Teri and at the other spa, which was owned by a woman who was battling alcoholism. I also saved money and paid all my bills and debts. This included a total of $3,500 for past-due traffic tickets, a fine for driving without insurance and registration, and a revoked license fee to get my driver's license back and my truck on the road.

During this clean time, I dated a man with liver disease. The affliction kept him sick, in and out of the hospital. I would rush to his rescue and cuddle with him to calm his fears. I promised to move with him to his home state of California, but when that time came, I sent him home on a bus and said I'd meet him in a few months. Right after he left, I took up seriously with a guy I'll call Dale.

I met Dale over dinner at a friend's house. At first sight, I fell in love. I found it hard to take my eyes off this man, all of nearly six feet tall, thin, with long brown hair, brown eyes, and tats all over—a gorgeous Italian-American. Plus he played guitar and sang! I started catching his performances at clubs. When he picked up his guitar and strummed, my heart fluttered. He had this weird sex appeal that I could not resist.

Soon, we were an item, but Dale had a drug problem and couldn't stay clean for anything. I would break things off with him because his drug use was putting negative pressure on my attempts to stay clean. In between our breakups, I'd date other guys, but ultimately, I'd always find myself back with Dale.

Suddenly one day, while at a bar where Dale was playing, the notion that I wanted to be "normal" popped into my head. I thought I could handle a little alcohol, a shot of Wild Turkey and a Heineken. So, I drank. I had been clean for thirteen months, but with those drinks, it was all downhill. Minutes afterward, I found the coke dealer in the bar and we were off to the races! Just like that, I was doing drugs like I had never stopped using them. I had been getting my life back, and boom, in a second, it was over. Just like that, I started shooting up coke again. Soon, I'd be doing heroin again too.

This would be no short relapse. It would last a year.

During this time, Dale and I got a small one-bedroom apartment. We had a month-to-month lease in a middle-class neighborhood in a Suffolk County town, interestingly enough, called Babylon, a term often used to suggest wickedness and corruption. We had a bed and a dresser in the bedroom and a TV in the living room, and that's about it.

While I dated Dale, I was still working my two jobs but wound up quitting the one with Teri before I completely destroyed it. I'd been shaking and throwing up and leaving work early. At one point, abscesses had also developed and blown up like balloons on my arms, a result of shooting up cocaine and heroin. They had popped and oozed white and green pus and left dime-sized scars.

I was fortunate to hang on to my other job. My other boss empathized with me because of her alcoholism. Though I'd come to work shaking from the drugs, she didn't fire me, but soon I wound up leaving that job anyway.

As you can surmise, neither Dale nor I were doing well financially. Consequently, we couldn't pay for our apartment and wound up having to move out of it after about a month and a half. Though Dale was a musician, he really made his money as a mechanic. He'd pick up jobs, then he'd lose them. Ironically, though we couldn't find money to pay for basic necessities, it seemed to be overflowing when we wanted to get tattoos; plus, we were fortunate because Dale's best friend, a tattoo artist, gave us discounts.

Dale liked women with tats. While we were together, I got my first one, on my right shoulder, a happy face with black X's for eyes and a red hanging tongue. It looked like a dead, or really wasted, man. Other tattoos would follow, including the symbol for my zodiac sign, Cancer, which looks like a sideways "69."

Without a roof over our heads, Dale and I wound up sleeping in my Durango for a week; and though we didn't have money for an apartment, we found ways to get drugs, including tricking dealers into thinking we'd paid them, say, $100. We'd do that by giving them a few one-dollar bills wrapped inside a ten-dollar bill—the equivalent of maybe $15—grabbing the drugs, and driving away. To buy basic necessities like food, I'd use bad checks.

Dale couldn't keep it together in his band either. Between sets, he and I would use drugs in the parking lot or restroom. If we weren't using in public restrooms, we'd do it in my truck, his car, and all over the streets of Brooklyn, where we had migrated to for the easy access to drugs.

Finally, I begged my mom to let us come home, and she opened her door. Disappointment and concern colored her face when she saw the two of us, both of us too thin and me with a strange cast to my skin. Mom's boyfriend at the time was pissed, to say the least, at the mess of a couple that had shown up on the doorstep. He didn't want Dale or me in the house. But Mom always wanted me safe, and if that meant allowing us to stay in her home, so be it. She knew that Dale and I were a package deal. She wasn't happy with the arrangement though.

I caught her rolling her eyes a few times and noticed that she began to stay at her boyfriend's house more often.

Mom figured out I was doing drugs again and, once again at a loss after all the help she had tried to give me, she reached out to my brothers to give them the update. Not long after Dale and I moved in with her, my oldest brother, Noah, called me from Denver to ask when I was going to kill myself because "you're doing it anyway, and you're torturing us all in the process." He told me to just end the suffering and pull the trigger or get my shit together. Of course, he didn't want me to die. He was just trying to make a point, and he was angry, with good reason.

Sometime in the midst of this season of my life, Mom booked a surprise trip for me and her to see Noah and Eli. Just the idea of being on a plane for hours without access to drugs made me sick. I tried to weasel my way out of the trip, but Mom was not having it. She wanted us to have a nice visit with my brothers, and, I'm sure, she hoped that they would counsel me on my drug use.

Since I couldn't get out of this trip and couldn't go for hours on end without getting high, I devised a plan to put small, and what I hoped would be undetectable, baggies of heroin under the elastic in my panties. It was winter 2003, and though I knew I'd be under intense scrutiny from airport security, as all passengers would be post 9/11, smuggling those drugs on the plane was a risk I felt I had to take. That's how much I "needed" drugs. I was willing to risk the possibility of imprisonment if it meant I could snort heroin in the airplane restroom to avoid getting dope sick.

My gamble paid off. As you know from the Introduction to this book, airport security put me through passenger checks, did not detect my baggies, and let me go to boarding.

As for my brothers, after Mom and I arrived in Denver they did in fact give me a hard talking-to about my revived drug use, but I did not want to hear them.

While I dated Dale, I overdosed, he overdosed, we got arrested, and I got really sick.

As for that overdose, it happened after my mom and I visited my brothers. It was the only one I would ever have. It started with a cocaine-induced grand mal seizure, which I had on my mother's couch before I lost consciousness. Mercifully, I came to. As I opened my eyes, I saw Dale standing over me with a phone in his hand, ready to call an ambulance. Through my haze, somehow I mustered the strength to say, "I love you." Afterward, I shot up more cocaine.

As messed up as we both were, Dale and I had become engaged. I proudly sported a tattoo, the Chinese symbol for love, on my ring finger, and so did he.

I could not wait to become his wife.

If you've relapsed more than once, you're never really sure when your commitment to kick drugs will really stick. So, years later, as I look back on my last day of using drugs, I can tell you that I had no idea it would be my last time.

Here's the scene: I sat in my mother's bathroom with blood running down my arms onto my clothes from shooting up heroin. My right side hurt. My skin gave off an unusual shade of yellow. I threw up uncontrollably. I cried hysterically as I looked in the mirror and saw myself staring back with black circles under my eyes. I looked at Dale and told him that I needed help, that I couldn't live like this anymore. Of course, after saying this, I shot up some more heroin with him. We used it all until we had none left.

The next day, in late January 2004, Dale left my house to stay with a friend and I called Benevolence Manor to pick me up. The person who took my call remembered me from my last stay there. A day later, a van arrived to take me to a detox center in upstate New York before my final journey to Benevolence.

For three long hours on the way to the detox facility, a young guy slept on the backseat while I sat up front with the driver, the only person besides me and the young guy in the van. The driver and I hardly said one word to each other. I preoccupied my mouth by puffing on a cigarette as I stared out the window with blank eyes. They gave no clue that I was scared.

So much was going through my mind. I knew that being weaned off drugs was going to make me sick, but I was also thinking that that sickness wouldn't be any worse than what I was already feeling. I was so tired, sad, lonely, nauseous, and totally and completely sick of myself. As the trees and other scenery flashed by from the window, I wondered why I kept on ending up doing drugs. I felt so sorry for myself and so angry at what I had become *again*. I pulled down a sun visor mirror and looked at the black circles under my eyes. Then, in shame, I covered my eyes with my hands.

After the long ride ended, I walked into the facility mentally, spiritually, emotionally, and financially broken. I didn't know if I was actually going to get clean and stay clean. After all, my track record sucked, but I was holding on to a hope that I could finally pick up the pieces of my life and change. For the first time, I was checking myself into rehab for me, not for my dog or because my mother made me. I was doing it for me.

After staff admitted me to the detox facility, I called Mom for the first time in days, surprising her. She hadn't been home when Dale and I were shooting up heroin in her bathroom or the next day when the van picked me up.

She was my mom, the only one I had, and I needed her and needed her to know how sick I was and know my plans.

"Mommy, I'm in detox. I'm safe," I said as I cried. "I need help. I don't want to do this anymore." In the midst of our talk, I could hear anxiety in Mom's voice as she said, "What's going to be different this time?" I told her that this time, everything was different, that I'd hit bottom before, but not like this. For the first time, I was scared I was going to die and become another statistic.

This was my fourth detox experience. I remember it like it happened yesterday. I felt like I was jumping out of my own skin. I was sweating and nauseous and had stomach cramps. My entire body was aching, crying out because I was so scared. I felt like something was crawling inside me. I was anxious, upset, fearful, and desperate because I wanted to use drugs, but I didn't want to have these feelings anymore. I was trapped between this contradiction and confusion. I was in a battle for my life. What was I going to do? Was I going to stay in detox and go to rehab, or was I going to run?

Medical staff put me on methadone, but it didn't do anything to take the edge off me. I had been taking an abundant mix of drugs daily and God knows how much of that included cocaine and heroin, so it didn't feel like the methadone was cutting through to help wean me off all those drugs. Maybe that was all in my head, so I knew I had to stay in detox and give it a chance to work. It was that or leave. Though I was upstate with no ride, I'm sure I could have figured out a way to escape—I'm very resourceful—but in my heart, I felt I was done. I was exhausted.

As I lay in a sparse room with another detoxing addict, I started having flashbacks: Of doing drugs with Dale. When Dale overdosed in a friend's house with her kid in the next room. Me saving Dale's life by calling an ambulance to take him to the hospital and getting arrested for it. The police handcuffing me to a hospital bed. I had to pee so bad, so they uncuffed me, but when I got to the restroom, not a drop came out. That happened to me a lot. I couldn't poop either, even when I felt the urge to do so badly. My body wasn't operating right. The drugs had taken over.

Ultimately, the charges the cops tried to slap on me for that incident didn't stick because I told a judge that the drugs Dale had taken weren't mine. I told him that I had saved Dale's life and that I wasn't an addict, so the judge let me go because I had no prior arrests.

But I would be arrested again. Dale and I were in Brooklyn in my Durango, doing heroin. Stupid me, I had left my bumper stickers with drug recovery expressions on the back of my truck. Cops were following us because they had spotted us shooting up, then they pulled us over with their guns out. They confiscated six bags of heroin from the truck, but they didn't take the needles. They cuffed us, put us in the back of the squad car, and took us to central booking.

Guards put me in a jail cell while I still wore my pajama pants and tank top, my outfit for the day because I had literally crawled out of bed in a friend's apartment to shoot up with Dale right before we were arrested. Central booking was freaking freezing, so let me tell you, with me in sheer sleeping clothes, the experience wasn't pleasant.

Authorities locked me away for nearly two days. In that time, I shared a toilet with a bunch of women who were crammed into one cell. I slept on the floor, snuggling with a cute lesbian because we were both cold. Those nearly two days jammed between cement walls and metal bars were long enough for me. I don't think I ever did any longer time than that in jail.

Officials released Dale and me on our own recognizance. I don't remember how we made it back to my truck that day, but somehow we did. We got in the Durango feeling dope sick and desperate, so very quickly we came up with another bright idea: rob our drug dealer. We asked him for a bundle of heroin, paid for it with our old trick of making a few dollars look like a hell of a lot more, snatched the heroin, and took off in the truck. We didn't stop until we hit junkie paradise, a gas station restroom where users were known to get high.

After five long days of replaying some of the worst moments of my life as I underwent detox, staff approved me for release from the facility. With that, I was ready to put my bad memories where they belonged: in the past. Following detox, I entered a twenty-eight-day rehab program, my third rehab experience, at Benevolence. It was February 2, 2004.

Before, I would have blamed everyone else for the mess that was my life: My father for dying. My brothers. My mother. I would have blamed the many men who had raped me. By this point, I understood that I had been raped. Cole was the boyfriend who had made that clear.

What I am about to say next will anger some people and may be viewed as controversial, but I have to speak my truth: I also realized that if I hadn't been on drugs, I wouldn't have been in compromising situations with so many guys in the first place. And if the guys hadn't been on drugs, they probably wouldn't have taken advantage of me. They might have not even realized what the fuck they were doing or maybe they did and they didn't care. Or maybe we all were on drugs and just didn't realize what we were doing or have the ability to think clearly or care. Whatever the case, that was then.

Over the span of my previous detox and rehab programs, a message had finally gotten through to me: I had volunteered for a lot of the bad things that had happened to me.

Having said this, I will be the first to say that rape is a crime. I'm not excusing what these guys did, but I knew I had to forgive them and myself or I would continue to suffer and never move on.

What I shared with you are just the facts. Once I realized the role I played in my problem, I also realized that I was the solution.

So, at age twenty-four, I was ready to get clean.

Now that I was on a mission to turn my life around, I had to figure out how to accomplish that. One thing I knew: I needed guidance because I couldn't do it alone.

At Benevolence, staff paired me with a counselor I had worked with during a previous rehab experience. She asked me what I was willing to do to stay clean. I responded, "Anything." I was the addict who was the life of the party growing up. I was always the party girl, always the girl who felt she had to prove she could do more drugs than anyone else and still stand. I'd had a death wish, and I hadn't even known it. The party girl who thought she was having so much fun had turned into a junkie, so when I told this woman "Anything," for the first time I saw my whole life flash in front of my eyes and I meant what I said.

That day with the counselor, I surrendered to a new, clean lifestyle. As the old saying goes, I was sick and tired of being sick and tired.

To find success in recovery, I realized that I needed to start truly listening to and following professional advice, so I hung on to every one of my counselor's words. She told me to begin attending twelve-step meetings during my stay at Benevolence and afterward, get some clean friends who could show me how to live without drugs . . . and without alcohol.

That meant I couldn't stay with Dale if he couldn't give up dope.

I wound up giving him an ultimatum: drugs or me. He chose drugs, so I ended our relationship. He loved being high more than he loved me. The old me understood where he was coming from. Four years before, Stephen had given me the same ultimatum, and I had chosen the thing that could kill me. The new me, however, never wanted to understand and embrace that mindset ever again.

With my renewed determination to stay clean, I had to face all the damage I had caused to myself and my loved ones, whom I had taken down emotionally, spiritually, and financially. I had to deal with my finances too. My credit was in the toilet. I owed $30,000 of my own credit card debt, not to mention all the money I owed to my mother, which was not limited to what I had stolen from her purse and credit cards. Mom had also taken out a home equity loan to pay for my Durango to prevent it from being repossessed. Then there was just the simple fact of earning her trust again.

About a month after completing my stay at Benevolence, my last rehab program, I began making headway on my debt because I went back to work. I had called my boss who struggled with alcoholism and asked for my old job back. I had promised her that I was really going to get my life in order, and she had agreed to rehire me. It helped that she was in recovery too. She understood my struggle and wanted to see me succeed.

I had also contacted my old boss, Teri, for whom I had worked at the spa in the gym. I promised her that I was going to stay clean this time, for real. She would take me back, she said, only because I was really good at my job when I wasn't using drugs. If I wanted to keep the job, she said, I'd have to keep my promise to not relapse.

I was determined to do just that. I had decided that I would stay off drugs no matter what. Every day, I would have to make the conscious decision to stick to that. I knew that the only way I could stay clean was to silence the inner voice that constantly lied to me, telling me that nothing is better than drugs, because the truth is that SO MUCH MORE IN THIS LIFE IS BETTER THAN DRUGS. A light at the end of the tunnel flamed, and that light was freedom—freedom from the destruction I am capable of doing to myself and the people I love. So, I couldn't give up or give in to the enemy within . . . no matter what happened.

PART THREE

RECOVERY

CHAPTER NINE

WALKING THE TWELVE STEPS

For what felt like all of my life, I hadn't known how to live clean because honestly, all I knew was to use. I was petrified to live *without* drugs, but months after being released from Benevolence for the last time, I discovered that I'd *have* to take them—just not the illegal kind—in order to live.

My health had dramatically deteriorated. I was constantly fatigued and vomiting, and it felt like someone was repeatedly sticking a knife in my right side. During these health struggles, I didn't see a medical professional. I feared knowing what was wrong.

When I finally got up the courage to see a doctor, he took one look at me then gave me a glance that said, *You need help. You're going to die.* He insisted that I get tested immediately. The idea terrified me because I had used dirty needles, dirty water, dirty cotton, dirty everything, and I had had unprotected sex with many people. I feared I might have HIV. But I followed his advice and got tested.

Thank God, the test showed I did not have HIV, but that was no reason to celebrate. It turned out that I was suffering from hepatitis C, a viral infection of the liver transmitted through blood. At twenty-four years old, my liver was failing.

Like a lightning bolt, the memory of how I likely got the disease struck me. Dale and I were getting high in my car with a woman who had hep C. Needles were strewn everywhere, and we didn't know whose were whose. I didn't care. I just wanted to get high. Our friend handed me a needle, and I stuck it into my vein. At that moment, I cared more about shooting up heroin and coke than my health, and that is the sad, honest truth. Now, I was paying an exorbitant price for that momentary high.

With the diagnosis, I hit an emotional and physical bottom that I had never touched before. At this time, hep C was more difficult to cure. The health industry would give you medicine that would make you terribly ill and hope the best for you. Maybe the medicine would work. Maybe it wouldn't.

As I struggled with my illness, I never felt so lonely, isolated, sick, and desperate. Yet I knew that I had to keep fighting. Fortunately, Mom had had my room waiting for me after my stay at Benevolence, so I had a clean and loving place to lay my head every night after long days of massage therapy work as I fought through my physical pain.

There was more. Mom monitored my hep C medicine. She made sure that I took only the prescribed doses, and she hid the medicine when it was not dosing time. Truthfully, there was no chance that I would sneak and take more of that horrible stuff because it made me feel so ill. But Mom wasn't taking any chances.

In the early days, every day of staying off illegal drugs proved to be a hard-won fight, a battle that was even tougher because I was also fighting hep C. At the time, I couldn't articulate my feelings about the pain the disease was causing or about my life in general, but the CD *How to Get Away with Murder* by rock group Papa Roach, spoke to, and for, me. That recording helped me get through my first year off drugs.

I'd be driving in my truck rocking out to Papa Roach's lyrics, so many of which I identified with as a person struggling to stay in recovery. When I felt the urge to get high, I'd sing along to their song "Done with You," which talks about missing someone while struggling with a liver problem and a broken heart. As I wailed that tune, I'd think about Dale choosing drugs over me and question why I was trying so hard to stay clean when I was probably going to die from hep C. The lyrics made me realize that many people were fighting drug addiction and physical illness, so if others could be victorious in this war, so could I.

As you can see, the battle to stay clean was a mental one. It was littered with questions about Dale, my health, and my future. It also had me wondering about my place in this world.

I constantly asked myself, "Who am I without drugs? Who is Marsha?"

I had no idea of the answer.

I had absolutely no identity. I didn't know my likes and dislikes. I didn't know if I was gay or straight; I had slept with a few women in the first months of being clean, looking for a substitute for the love I no longer shared with Dale. Confusion, frustration, and sadness enveloped me. I didn't know how to be social without drugs or how to have sex without them. My feelings were scattered. I was a lost soul, and I needed someone, anyone, to show me how to live without drugs because I didn't know how.

My counselor at Benevolence had suggested I get a sponsor. I followed her advice and found someone that I could hang with and confide in. Suddenly, I was sharing shit with one person that I wouldn't want to share with anyone. I told her everything I had been capable of doing when I had used drugs and what I thought I was capable of doing while clean. That took courage because I didn't have a lot of faith in people.

I met my sponsor through a step program in a church basement on Long Island not far from my childhood neighborhood. In these meetings, on any given day, I'd be among twenty to fifty people, sometimes even more, with struggles similar to my own. In particular,

I looked up to the survivors of addiction who shared their success stories and suggestions about how to stay clean.

These survivors talked about how the twelve steps could give you freedom from active addiction. I would walk the steps and find that what they had said was true. The steps would help me differentiate between diseased thinking and reality and give me hope that I could stay clean if I was willing to do the work.

I was now more than willing, and twelve steps began to show me the way.

What follows is my version of the twelve steps. Here, I share each and every one of them to help you better understand my story:

1. *I surrender to the fact that I have gotten completely out of control and unmanageable and admit that I can't do this anymore.*
2. *I must look to a higher power to restore my sanity in order to successfully receive help.*
3. *I must turn my life over to the God of my understanding.*
4. *I must investigate my past actions and be honest about them.*
5. *I must come clean to God, another person, and myself about my past.*
6. *I must surrender to God to eradicate my character flaws.*
7. *I must beseech God to make my character flaws history.*
8. *I must identify the people I have hurt and be open to improving relationships with them.*
9. *I must follow through on improving those relationships unless doing so would be counterproductive.*
10. *I must continue to analyze my actions and be honest about them after I have done something wrong.*

11. *I must pray to God for guidance.*
12. *I must try to help other addicts by spreading the positive messages I have learned about redemption and recovery as a result of walking the twelve steps.*

Twelve-step recovery literature says that some of us have a hard time getting over active addiction because we think we are too cool. For a long time, that was me. I had to become completely humiliated, knocked down from my "perch" with the "cool kids," to ask for help. Now that I had the willingness to do whatever I needed to do to recover, I began to follow the steps religiously. Slowly but surely, I worked through each one of them, answering tough questions about myself in a twelve-step workbook and sharing my responses with my sponsor. This forced me to be honest with myself, and I began to change my life.

Steps five, six, and seven were the hardest to master. I flinched when I took a real, hard look in the mirror at my past actions (step five). And I had to get to a point where I was completely aware of what I had been doing so that I could ask God to remove my character flaws (steps six and seven). By the time you get to those two steps, you're ready to change for the good.

With my sponsor's help, during step six I discovered that my character flaws numbered thirty.

That number slapped me in the face. Among my flaws: I was resentful toward everyone, including myself. I was spiteful; if someone hurt me, I'd say or do something to hurt them back. I was lustful, impulsive, filled with self-pity, and dishonest. Often, I was angry for no valid reason. And I'll end this list, which as you know is far more extensive, by saying that I always had to be in control. I always felt like I needed the upper hand in all of my relationships and in my life in general. God forbid that I let anyone help me or get into my heart.

Confronting my flaws made me uncomfortable. I didn't like what they said about me. I told my sponsor, who had helped me create the list, "So basically, you're telling me I'm an asshole." She told me that I was being too hard on myself and encouraged me to look at my assets too. They included being loving, caring, compassionate, understanding, loyal, hardworking, strong, resilient, and not being a gossip. I am grateful to my sponsor for making me recognize these assets because I needed that positivity to keep pushing through the program.

This all leads me to the seventh step, beseeching God to make my character flaws history. In short, the more step work I performed, the more I became aware of how my character flaws were controlling my life. This made me even more uncomfortable with myself, which made me determined to do more step work.

In the course of that work, I discovered that my flaws all have antonyms, so when I felt *resentful*, I took a deep breath and prayed to feel *content* and for *forgiveness*. When I felt *spiteful*, I countered that by deciding to be a *better person* by embracing and acting on the idea that just because someone has hurt me does not mean that I have to hurt them. I could be kind and *walk away* with dignity and grace. And when I got *angry*, I *took a deep breath* and tried to *laugh things off.* I countered *dishonesty* with *honesty*. As for *control*, I stepped back and *acknowledged that I had never been in control* anyway, then I prayed and gave my feelings to the universe, my higher power. Now, am I perfect with all of this? No. It is a daily practice, and I have gotten better, but I am only human after all.

But back to this concept of a higher power.

The second step calls for the necessity of seeking out a higher power in order to restore your sanity. Some people call that power "God." Step three calls for turning your life over to the God of your understanding. When I began the twelve steps, I didn't know what God meant to me so I didn't understand him. Then one day I experienced an epiphany: God is that feeling in my gut about doing the right thing. Every time I get a knot in my stomach that tells me something is wrong—whether it's dating the wrong person, eating too much food, wanting to reach for drugs—that's God talking to me, trying to get me to live in his will to be a better person.

I began to understand that when I ignore God's will, I will stay sick, make bad decisions, and get in trouble, whereas when I act according to God's will, I will live in the spirit of love, peace, and forgiveness. For a long time, I did the wrong thing but was not able to stop. But once I had spirituality, a higher power, I *was* able to hit the brakes.

I don't believe in organized religion, but I do believe in living by spiritual principles. A spiritual life calls for doing "the next right thing," a phrase we hear often in twelve-step meetings. That right thing, for me, is loving my neighbor, being a good person, a better person. God does not want me to harm myself and other people. That's not God. That's what the twelve steps is about; it is a God-centered way of journeying through life that helps us become better people, frees us from negative aspects of our pasts, and helps us understand that we are different people than the active addicts we had once been. It is a way to help us live in the spirit of God, trust our conscious, and do the next right thing.

Walking the steps was like hiking the steepest mountain. I accomplished every long, laborious one with enormous effort and will. Along the way, I made many amazing friends, and today I continue to meet with a step group that I talk with openly. The meetings have helped me change my life.

In the early days, I attended get-togethers in church basements all over New York City as well as on Long Island because my life depended on it. In addition to the meetings, I ran with some of the people I met in the groups in an effort to stay on the right path. We literally racked up miles running on trails and the streets. Not only did I get physically stronger, as the years progressed my recovery got stronger as well.

It truly happened one day at a time, one step at a time. I couldn't run away from life just because I had decided to get clean. I had to get right with myself, accept who I am, and do enough step work so that I could live comfortably in the outside world. I had to do this so that, for instance, when I went to dinner with family and friends who might be drinking, I'd be cool. Same if they wanted to drink at concerts and shows. I couldn't stop going out because of everyone else or expect them to not drink—or smoke pot—just because I didn't.

I started to learn how to live a day at a time without drugs. Eventually, I could attend family parties, bat mitzvahs, weddings, and other functions and dance and laugh and have the best time and do it without a drink or a drug without having an anxiety attack. I had to learn how to take my recovery with me everywhere I went. That includes when I revisited that psychologist who had refused to see me again until I got clean and wouldn't nod off in session. At my mother's urging, I sat down and talked with him once weekly for a year a few years after my last rehab stay.

In this second wave of therapy sessions, I learned that not only do I have an addictive personality but that I also suffer from a strong tendency to seek unstable relationships and from body dysmorphic disorder, a condition in which the sufferer continually focuses on a real or imagined physical flaw. The doctor prescribed medicine to help me, but I refused to fill the prescription. I wanted to get mentally healthy by changing how I think, not by swallowing a pill. By this point, I had finished taking the hep C medicine—I'll share more about this in a minute. At any rate, not taking drugs for my psychological problems was the right choice for me at the time, as it helped me stay on the straight and narrow and off drugs.

However, I have not been perfect with substance use since getting clean. So, I have to "come clean" about something: In the first years of my recovery, even for a while when I was suffering from hep C, I smoked about a pack of cigarettes a day to fight the urge to use illegal drugs. I'm not proud of this, especially in light of my father's fatal addiction to cigarettes, but for someone like me who had smoked crack, they were the lesser of two evils. That said, today I smoke the occasional cigarette or cigar socially or sometimes when I'm ultrastressed, but that's about it. I'm still not proud of that, but smoking fewer cigarettes is progress for me because back in the day, I felt I needed them constantly to help me get to a better place.

When all is said and done, whatever it took, I'm forever grateful I got off illegal drugs. I became a better person, the version of myself that the universe always wanted me to be.

I picked up the pieces of my life and put the puzzle that is me back together. I changed. I got my family's trust back. I nurtured my career. I became spiritually centered, and a higher power has helped me stay on the right track. As for my hep C, I took a cocktail of interferon and ribavirin for eleven months after my diagnosis, and it took me years to recover. Progress came too late for me. Today, there's an eight-week cure for hep C. I encourage people to get the help they need if they have the disease.

CHAPTER TEN

DIVIDENDS OF RECOVERY

Recovery comes with many side benefits. For me, one dividend has been Reiki, the Japanese practice of healing with your hands that I learned a bit about in the early days of my massage therapy career. Four years after getting clean, I went back to my old Reiki Master for private master classes and soon found my knowledge of Reiki growing exponentially.

Practicing Reiki calmed me. It also changed how I presented myself to the world. Instead of adorning myself with combat boots to wage my fight with everyday life, I donned crystals around my neck and on my fingers and wrists. I believe crystals intensify my good, natural energy and help me practice at my optimum level as I work on people on the massage table.

I began to make other changes. My number of tattoos eventually grew to ten. They became reflective of who I was becoming. That stupid smiley face with the tongue hanging out and X's for eyes that I got when I dated Dale? Now, a beautiful image of a purple lotus flower with yellow petals blooms in its place. Other tats include symbols for faith and hope on my left wrist and, on my right wrist, the infinity symbol with the Reiki symbol for love above it. On my inner left arm I also have a quote that summarizes my life: *"Stand for something or fall for anything."*

I now stand for trying to do the next right thing every day of my life.

Another great benefit of recovery: It can open your eyes to help you see the good that's always been around you. For instance, I found that the longer I stayed clean, I could see God in many people I encountered.

Among them:

Ezra. He is the most amazing man. Ezra lost his seventeen-year-old daughter to a car accident years before we met. He didn't have his daughter, and I didn't have my father. It was like the universe put us in each other's lives to save a piece of ourselves. I can't speak for Ezra, but that's how I feel.

Ezra appeared in my life as a client at one of the day spas I worked for when I was at the height of my active addiction. He could tell I had a problem and instantly offered his friendship. From Ezra, I learned that I can rely on a man and depend on someone to help, guide, and love me without there being a catch. He never asked anything of me except that I get well. I was so young when my father died that I never learned how a man is supposed to treat a woman. But Ezra began to change that.

For nearly two decades now, he has sent me flowers on my birthday. He has given me financial gifts and just fun things; but the most important gift he has given me is showing me unconditional love and support. It's all been from the goodness of his heart, no expectations. Our relationship has never been anything but platonic. He is happily married and just wants to show me that I can be anything I want to be if I just have faith in myself. He has always shown up for me, encouraged me, and listened to me. My eyes only fully recognized the beautiful friendship Ezra offered me after I got clean.

A Police Officer I Worked on at a Massage Spa. The day he walked in, I did a double take. He looked so familiar. As I massaged his back, he mentioned his patrol area, and then I knew I had encountered him in my time on the streets. I smiled inside and replayed the memory: He took my car to the impound lot because I had rented it out to drug dealers. Then he brought my stuff from my car to my mom. In the midst of all of this, I was missing in action. Mom begged him to arrest me if he found me, and he told her he hadn't caught me in an illegal act, so there was nothing he could do; but he assured her that I was alive and okay.

For several weeks at the spa, I worked on the officer before I got up the nerve to tell him that we'd met when I was in active addiction. He hadn't figured out who I was because I looked so different; but after I revealed my identity, he smiled. He said he was so happy that I was clean. I would work on him a few more times, all the while feeling grateful that my higher power had put him back on my path so that I could thank him.

Painter. During my battle with hep C, I writhed in pain on the floor at Painter's house from the vicious side effects of the interferon and ribavirin. Painter, a big biker dude who loves his Harleys, saved my life by simply being there for me. He understood that I needed support beyond my sponsor and other recovery friends. He came into my life through the twelve-step program and took me under his wing almost immediately. I became a regular at his house, where he ran his own step group and where he and his wife and kids hosted dinners for friends.

He took me for rides on the back of his motorcycle and to picnics. His wife and kids loved me like I was a member of the family too. In a sense, they all loved me back to health. They wanted nothing from me but that I stay clean and get better.

Autumn. This long-haired, bubbly redhead walked in on me while I was stretching in pain on Painter's floor. In a happy voice, she asked me if I had a problem. "I'm sick," I told her. From that moment, Autumn, who was attending meetings at Painter's house too, offered me unconditional friendship. She taught me what true love and friendship are all about. Despite both of our many ups and downs, we would be there for each other, and a mutual love of rock music—Papa Roach, Alice in Chains, and so many other bands and concerts—has strengthened our bond.

Autumn is a big crier, and I asked her why. She told me that crying allows us to feel, deal, and heal. I took this great lesson to heart, and it helped me tremendously years later. And while Autumn helped me, I would later help her, by becoming her sponsor. She always says I saved and changed her life. Little does she know how much she saved and changed mine.

One of the most beautiful aspects of recovery is that it puts you in a frame of mind to help other people who suffer from addiction. Months after becoming clean, I began sharing inspiring messages of hope at rehab centers and step meetings, and after a year, my higher power led me to become a sponsor to many women like Autumn as well. At the time of this writing, I have sponsored at least forty women.

I am so pleased to say that I have numerous success stories in sponsorship. I've taken many women through the steps who have remained clean, some having achieved as long as fifteen years off drugs.

Sponsorship has also helped *me* because it keeps me in recovery. It keeps me honest. It keeps me in step work and going to meetings and answering the phone even when I don't want to. It keeps me showing up for people even if I'm not in the mood. I may be watching Netflix and don't feel like putting the movie on pause, but I do it anyway, although sometimes I call the person back shortly after the movie is over. Laugh out loud! I'm not perfect, ya know!

But anyway, I've got to stay clean for me *and* because I love helping others. I want to continue to be there for them. Right now, I am sponsoring five amazing women whom I love dearly. They trust me with everything, and that is a true honor. It's amazing to watch someone come into recovery so beaten and broken and emerge to do step work to turn their life around. It's a priceless gift to see their transformation. So just for today, I won't allow any amount of drugs to take that feeling away. It's not just about me anymore, and it never was.

About five years after getting clean, my recovery work expanded from sponsoring women and talking to small groups to appearing at large twelve-step conventions. I say this when I speak all the time now: "As long as there is still a breath in your body you still have a chance to change and save your life because it's not over until it's over. The ultimate bottom is death—no more chances and no more choices." I have shared this message at twenty twelve-step conventions on the East Coast in front of hundreds of people. I've opened my life to others on topics like staying clean and living dirty, self-acceptance, recovery equals discovery, and making amends to the people you've harmed.

CHAPTER ELEVEN

ADDICTION'S TOLL

When I think of my life story, I know that I might not have had a chance to write it. Many of the addicted people I knew while growing up suffered that fate: They never told their stories because they succumbed to the disease of addiction.

Some of these friends were the "cool kids" I hung out with while growing up. Some of them died before the age of thirty; some died as teenagers from overdoses, suicides, car accidents, shootings, and other adventures of misfortune related to using drugs.

Lannie died at about age thirty-three. I'm not sure if it was drug related, but I have my suspicions.

The guy on the floor with Lannie the night of my rape died at around age twenty-nine.

Luke, the man who raped me, died of an overdose in his thirties.

Layne, the friend who accompanied Eli and me at the infamous rave in Brooklyn, was found dead of an overdose in his twenties. At one point, Layne had practically lived at our house. He had claimed he had a rough family life, so he'd given us drugs in exchange for a safe place to stay. He had accepted other people's protection, but ultimately, he couldn't protect himself.

There are others I haven't previously mentioned. A friend named Daryl, who smoked crack, hanged himself in his early twenties. Louis, also in his early twenties, overdosed on heroin, and his parents found him dead. Another friend of mine, Bruce, in his late forties, overdosed on heroin too. A friend and I identified his body then went to his mother's house to give her the news. I will never forget the devastation on her face.

Another one of my close friends had a stroke in her early fifties after years of cigarette addiction. She chain-smoked despite a heart condition and left behind two kids and a husband. Sound familiar? Yes, it sounds like my family. My friend lay in a hospital bed on a ventilator. After staff pulled the plug, I held her hand until she took her last breath.

Then there is Paul B. I'm going to spend a few extra words on him because he was one of my closest friends.

Paul had twelve years clean and sponsored countless people. A horrific motorcycle accident, however, would shatter his track record. He almost lost a leg. Consequently, he underwent numerous surgeries and a doctor put him on prescription opioids. That left him with the urge to use again. He relapsed. He began shooting up heroin and coke and smoking crack.

At a step meeting sometime later, Paul fell into my arms and smelled my neck. My favorite perfume, Egyptian Musk, rose from my skin and into the air around me, comforting him. Paul sighed in relief. "You always smell the same," he told me as we hugged each other tight.

During the meeting, Paul admitted to relapsing. I and others offered him help, but he said he was managing, that he was okay. Repeatedly, he rebuffed our offers. His denial would be his undoing.

About two years after his accident, Paul's drug use caught up with him. He died of an overdose of heroin that was cut, I deeply suspect, with the illicit version of the opioid fentanyl. Fentanyl is a drug up to 100 times stronger than morphine, and many reports have cited the illegal version of it as the primary driver of drug overdose deaths in the US overall. Paul didn't mean to die. I'm sure he thought he could get away with using drugs just one more time and come out fine, but he didn't. I learned of his death just two days after talking to him on the phone. We had shared how much we loved and appreciated each other and couldn't wait to see each other that weekend. But just like that, he was gone.

The news of Paul's death dropped me to my knees on my living room floor. I cried and screamed "no" over and over.

Paul and I had been more than just people who knew each other in recovery. No, not boyfriend and girlfriend, though many people thought we would have made a great couple. No, we were truly great friends. We shared some of our most intimate secrets with each other.

Of all of my many platonic guy friends, only Paul had looked at me with a searing intensity that went beyond words. We were close, literally. When we weren't dating others, we would sometimes sleep together, cuddle, laugh, and be emotionally intimate. We tried to have sex once, but we didn't get very far, probably because neither of us wanted to ruin our friendship. Remaining friends was more important to us than having a romance.

Despite our closeness, however, there was nothing I could say or do to help Paul after his relapse. He was just too far gone, too far to be reached. Now, he is gone forever.

The day he died, many hearts broke. He left behind a son, a young man who he was extremely proud of, and many friends, family members, and people he had touched in recovery.

So many more people I know have died due to drug- and addiction-related incidents—so many, I can't count. One of them was the son of my doctor who diagnosed my hep C. He died of a heroin overdose. As you can see, the disease of addiction does not care about your family background or your station in life. It does not care who you are.

The disease of addiction is self-centered too. It doesn't care about anyone else. Once we get it, all bets are off. We become different people. It's as if another entity takes us over. The person who you knew is no longer that happy-go-lucky, fun-filled person.

He or she becomes a manipulative, lying, scheming individual and doesn't care about anything except getting the next one. We don't think about how our addiction can affect others.

That brings me to one last story. Among the people I've lost to addiction is a good friend who had HIV, hep C, and cancer. She was beautiful inside and out, a gorgeous woman in her thirties who couldn't stay clean and, ultimately, threw herself in front of a train, devastating many people. You have to be in a lot of pain to do that. I stood in front of her casket and couldn't even cry. I believed that if I started to cry, the floodgates would open and I would never stop.

Several years passed before I could shed a tear. Then, I allowed myself to cry every day for a month and release my pain. I had held in my tears for so long that it was freeing to let them go. Autumn had been right about the power of crying. It certainly does allow you to feel, deal, and heal.

As the tears poured, I thought of my friend and fully appreciated the fact that I was on earth to cry at all. I thanked God's mercy for that.

I say I released my pain, and at that time, I really thought I had. But as more years passed, I realized that a lot more pain had been bottled up inside me. Recently, I released a wellspring of it. To get there, I had to go through three rounds of the step program, answering questions in my workbook about my actions and motivations, to cry from the past hurt and my behavior patterns that stemmed from years of abuse, neglect, and abandonment.

I hadn't really allowed myself to deeply feel and heal until that moment that I finally truly let my tears flow. My sponsor helped lead me to this point. She had been crying for me, and I had asked her why. She had asked me why I *wasn't* crying. I shot her a confused look.

Often in recovery, we talk about how we had to get clean to learn what addiction is truly about. One of the lessons we learn: Once you're an addict, you're always an addict. That lesson has certainly held true for me. After being off drugs for years, I discovered that I still had a problem. It was the problem my sponsor was crying about: I was a love addict.

Dealing with feelings and emotions we've never faced can be hard and painful, and I don't know about anyone else, but those feelings were making me act out of character. Whenever a guy broke my heart, I wanted to fix it with another feeling or a person or thing, like sex or an unhealthy relationship. I call that a "love" addiction, not a sex addiction, because I was seeking to fill an emotional, not a physical, void.

With that said, the trigger for my love addiction getting out of control was a long-term relationship that ended.

CHAPTER TWELVE

LOSING IT AND GETTING IT TOGETHER

Julian.

Where do I begin?

I was six months clean and taking medicine for hep C the day our eyes met in a rehab facility. As I spoke words of encouragement to a group, I spotted this tall, dark man with sideburns. It was like love at first sight or addiction at first sight. Only one other time in my life had I experienced the feeling that overwhelmed me in that moment. That other time occurred when I met Dale.

My relationship with Julian, another gorgeous Italian-American man, started about a year and a half after our first encounter and lasted longer than any I had ever had—five years. It began when I was twenty-six.

Julian once had a bad drug habit but, like me, was in recovery. He and I connected in a deep way. He was an amazing keyboardist and drummer. And oh, I loved it when he sang! The two of us were crazy for music. We attended concerts all over New York—Billy Joel, Linkin Park, the Allman Brothers. Those are just the ones I remember. We hung out with his big Italian family a lot, traveling with them to Disney World and elsewhere too.

We shared the same spiritual beliefs. Like me, Julian felt that a higher power guides us all if we will only heed it. We laughed together a lot, cried together a lot, and supported each other.

Julian taught me what it is to truly make love to a man. I had had a hard time looking into a man's eyes while being sexually intimate. Shit, I had been emotionally detached for so long that I had had a hard time looking into *anyone's* eyes. Julian used to say, "Look at me," and I'd cry. Sometimes, the energy and passion between us exploded. In the beginning, nothing mattered more than being with him.

But the relationship began to suffocate me.

Julian was jealous, controlling, and insecure. He hated that I had a couple of guy friends; all of them were strictly platonic. He'd drive me nuts if I didn't pay attention to him at a step meeting because I was focused on people I sponsored or friends. I'd have to console him and let him know that it was okay that I wasn't with him for the entire meeting, or at the coffee shop, the bar where he was performing, the restaurant, and on and on.

If I wasn't right there by Julian's side the whole time, he would freak out. I'd be having a good time in the back of the bar with my friends, and he'd come find me and pick a fight with me because of it. He knew he was being irrational, but he couldn't control himself.

Thoughts of leaving him entered and exited my mind. He had made me part of his family, a type of belonging I had sought since my father died, and I loved it. His parents adored me, but they also knew that their son could be emotionally abusive. At the three-year mark in our relationship, his mom sat me down and told me the family would understand if I chose to leave him. I thanked her, but I stayed with Julian. It continued to be a bumpy ride.

Julian couldn't hold a job. In the years we were together, he was fired from too many to count. Meanwhile, I was holding down several jobs, lived with my mom, saved money, and was taking those private classes to become a Reiki Master.

At some point, I moved out of Mom's house and rented an apartment. I paid for it with my earnings from what were now three jobs at massage spas, yet Julian was making no personal or professional progress. I didn't understand why he just couldn't get his act together, so

I began pulling away from him . . . and he became even more insecure. We began to grow apart. In response to the stress of the relationship, I ate handfuls of cookies and other bad food and put on thirty-five unwanted pounds . . . and began to hate myself.

Our relationship wasn't all bad. Julian adored me and was very affectionate. I'm sure he never cheated on me, and never once did I cheat on him. He showed me off to his friends and was proud to be with me. I loved him beyond measure. But the bad outweighed the good.

I am a free spirit, and a lot of men can't handle that. Maybe it's me, maybe it's them, or maybe I just haven't found the right person. As for Julian, the more I grew in recovery, the more he and I grew apart, though we both desperately held on to each other.

In the last year of our relationship, I went through so many changes, including losing my precious dog, Heidi, whom I had adopted when she was nearly two years old. Though she was only expected to live to age five because of her liver disease, she made it to eleven. After I got clean, I had been religious about her care, giving her medicine three times a day, feeding her special food, and massaging her. Since she and I both had liver problems, we had a real kinship. By the end of her life, the vet had said she was practically living without a liver and that she believed my love and nurturing had kept her alive.

The day I let Heidi go was one of the hardest of my life. Eight people showed up in the vet's office to be with me. That's a testament to being in recovery; it provides you with a wealth of friends who truly care. As I was about to say goodbye to Heidi, I looked around and saw my mom, her new boyfriend, and five of my best friends from step meetings. Julian was there too. In Heidi's last moments, he held me so tight. His love and support made me think that maybe we could make our relationship work.

For a few months after Heidi's death, things seemed to be going well between Julian and me. Our fighting ceased. We were trying to make things right.

While things were going well for a stretch with Julian, I was excelling in my massage therapy job at the gym, where I had once worked for Teri but now worked for a woman named Gail, the new owner. I credit my professional progress to becoming a more spiritual person the longer I stayed clean. Adorned in crystals, I found my great joy and peace as I performed Reiki or deep tissue massage on clients to help them heal or simply feel better.

At some point, I quit working at the other two spas to focus exclusively on my job with Gail. I had become tired of all the travel between the facilities, which was counterproductive to what I really wanted to do: build a strong clientele at one business. Sometimes, I had run back and forth between the three businesses several times a day.

My love of massage was evident to Gail, who saw it not only with her own eyes but heard about it from my clients too. Then sometime after switching allegiances to work for her only, she announced that she was moving upstate. In the next second, she asked me if I would be interested in buying her spa. I practically screamed, "Yes!"

Now, more than half a decade after getting clean, Gail was offering to sell me the business that Teri had welcomed me back to with trepidation but also with hope that I'd stay in recovery. I had fulfilled that hope, performed my job well, and had indeed built a loyal and bustling clientele. Gail recognized all of this and told me that I was a natural to run the spa.

I felt I could make the place great too, and I was ready! Gail practically cheered when I told her I wanted to take her up on her offer; she wouldn't have the time and energy to focus on her business after her move.

Before I knew it, Gail greenlighted the sale and signed the business over to me. I paid her a small fee for her office furniture and equipment, and with that, I made the best investment of my life.

I celebrated becoming a business owner with my brothers, who, by this point, had moved back to New York. I don't remember why, but Julian did not accompany us that night. At our celebration, in a restaurant, we sat at a bar as we waited for a table to become available. The bartender, a family friend, put a free drink in front of me, which rattled my already stressed-out nerves. Thoughts of taking on a business had made me elated and sad all at once; this needled my addiction core. I found myself picking up the drink, smelling it, putting it down, picking it up, putting it down. For the first time since becoming clean about six years before, I found myself really, really wanting to drink. My brothers looked at me with fear but said nothing.

Let me tell you, I scared the shit out of myself that night, but I didn't take that drink. Instead, the next day I hightailed it to a meeting. A great new life awaited me, and I didn't want to do anything to destroy it.

Over the years, I had learned something heavy about myself: I'm not a person who can have "just one" of anything. I mean, maybe I *could* have just one drink or smoke a little pot, but what if I couldn't stop at that? Honestly, it was not worth going down that road to even answer the question. I didn't need drugs or alcohol to have a good time or to loosen up, so why bother? I had way too much to lose and way too many people who depended on me and loved me. I was not going to let them down. Yes, I had come that far in my thinking by the time I bought the spa.

Quickly, I found that owning a business is a big responsibility, and it scared me out of my mind. Sometimes, my diseased thinking would say to me, "You can't do this. You aren't good enough. You don't deserve this. There's no way you will be successful." I knew my thoughts weren't rational. I had done enough self-work to know how to differentiate between diseased thinking and reality, so I told the itty-bitty shitty committee in my head to shut the fuck up and I got to work.

I put the business in my name and incorporated it. I hired an accountant, had a friend make a website for me, got my advertising going, and connected with a physical therapist, chiropractors, doctors, attorneys, personal trainers, and other business owners. I talked to everyone and anyone for tips about how to be successful.

In the early months of the business, I paid Julian to help me. For instance, I gave him twenty dollars to bring my laundry up to my office. Julian's willingness to take the money disappointed me. Boyfriends are just supposed to do that stuff for you. I shouldn't have had to pay the dude. He was broke and unemployed, so I was trying to help when really I was acting codependent and insane. In turn, I felt *angry* and *resentful* about the whole relationship. And no, I didn't lean on the twelve steps to find antonyms to counter these feelings. I'm human and don't always do things by the book. It didn't help that Julian constantly lured me into fights too, draining what little energy I had after a full day at work.

There was more. They say that when you take over a business you are married to it in the beginning, and I can tell you that's true. My business became my life. Making money and becoming successful became more important to me than Julian, my recovery, friendships, and my family. My goal: a successful business and financial freedom.

Don't misunderstand me. I still attended meetings, hung out with friends and family, sponsored people in twelve steps, and rocked out at concerts, but I worked more than I did any of that. Mom had taught me that the only person I can depend on is me, and she was right. You never know what can happen in life; people die, people leave, so you have to know how to stand on your own feet. I never wanted anyone to say that if it wasn't for them, I wouldn't have the life I enjoyed.

During this time of personal and professional growth, I also realized that a loving, caring relationship should flow naturally, not be a constant struggle like Julian and I shared. Finally, the day of reckoning came after Julian accused me in front of a bunch of New Year's partygoers of flirting with another guy. I had had it with the struggle. That night, I told him that we were over.

He knew our relationship was done, yet he kept saying he couldn't believe I was breaking up with him. But after five years together, I definitely did.

Walking away from Julian hurt me. I still wonder how things would be had we remained a couple. But we can't live in the world of what ifs, if onlys, and all we wants.

Julian wasn't a bad guy. We just didn't meet at the right time. He's with the person he's supposed to be with now, and I'm running my business and sitting here writing this book, which is what I'm supposed to be doing.

CHAPTER THIRTEEN

THE DISEASE OF ADDICTION

Being in recovery doesn't mean "you've got it all together." You must be vigilant to remain on a good course. It's not just about staying clean or staying sober or not overeating or not overspending anymore. It can also be about making sure you don't replace your old addiction with another one or let a lingering addiction take over. Sometimes, giving up one addiction can lead to another one grabbing center stage.

That's what happened to me after I broke up with Julian. While I had put my drug addiction to rest, my love issues came back to the forefront. I didn't know how to handle my feelings and I didn't want to go back to using drugs, so I did something destructive: I had indiscriminate sex with multiple partners like I had done years before.

So many times, I had sex with someone before I got to know them, then shortly afterward, I'd realize I didn't even like them. Then suddenly, I would become a shit show wondering, *How the hell am I going to get out of this nightmare?* Once, before Julian, I had sex with three men and two women at the same time at a swingers club. We used condoms, but nevertheless, my behavior was insane.

I was the type of person who thought that others were replaceable. I floated in and out of crowds not allowing people to get close.

I was a scared little girl who just wanted to feel safe and loved all the time. But she was too scared—scared that she'd lose love once she found it, like my mother had. She thought it would be ripped away from her because the person might die or choose to simply leave.

I feared that people would realize just how broken I was inside and wouldn't fully accept me for the beautiful disaster that was me.

I chose men who weren't stable, loyal, or honest and couldn't be the man I needed them to be. I attracted sick people because I am a healer. Yes, water seeks its own level, so my fear of commitment kept me with people that I knew I couldn't have a future with.

My men were emotionally or physically abusive, and in turn, I met their behavior and became someone I am not. I blamed them for my choices because I didn't want to deal with the past hurts of sexual, mental, and physical abuse, and I fell deeper and deeper into a black hole of anger and resentment. Then I ignored those feelings and did not find their antonyms. As a result, I kept repeating the same behavior.

After my relationship with Julian ended, I discovered that sex was still like a drug for me. Just like when I was a teen, it numbed me. It was a poor replacement for what I really wanted: a loving, caring relationship. Though I was in my thirties, I was still trying to fill a void that had been left in my soul when my dad died. I hadn't made much emotional progress on this front at all!

Here I had once been a junkie with no hope, driving around every day in a truck with no heat in the middle of winter while shooting up heroin and cocaine, an empty shell of a human being crying daily from misery, vomiting every day, and getting sick with every shot of drugs I took because I had hepatitis C, though I didn't know it, vomiting constantly because I'd subjected my body to an onslaught of drugs, having to use them just to wake up to get a start to my day, and was in recovery from this and now here I was in a bad bed of my own making *again*.

Though I had managed to stay clean, somehow my self-esteem and self-respect remained in the toilet. Somehow, a voice in my head was still telling me that I wasn't good enough. Consequently, I was getting involved with the wrong kind of men.

They included:

- Jack, two months (I went out with him shortly after I got my heart broken by this guy Alex.)
- Chuck, three months (He had seven years clean and was fresh out of a five-year relationship. I should have known not to get involved with a rebounder, but I hooked up with him anyway and I got hurt.)
- Landon, five months (He was a chronic relapser. We fought like cats and dogs. He'd choke me, and I'd choke him.)
- Dale, three months (Yes, I got back with him for a short while. He was clean in the beginning but relapsed while we were together.)
- Lucas, two months (He was a guy I knew from high school who turned out be a drug dealer.)
- Somewhere in the midst of this I hooked up with Cole again for a bit. Like Dale, he was clean when we reunited, but he relapsed not long afterward.

Many of the men I got involved with were the same type I had been attracted to when I was on drugs. Also, I had sex with men I barely knew and did not use a condom. I went online to find partners, men who were complete strangers, and went to their houses. They visited me at my place too.

At one point, I tested positive for the human papillomavirus, a sexually transmitted infection that can result in various cancers, including cervical and oral cancer. Recent test results show no traces of the virus in my system, but the fact that I put myself at risk for it still makes my head spin. I've had countless stalkers too. You know, scary shit—years of misery, heartache, and insanity.

As I look back at all of this, it shocks me that I allowed it to go on for so long.

I am a success story. I remain in recovery and am a successful business owner, yet the fact is *I'm an addict.* As I have said repeatedly in this book, addiction is a disease. It does not go away. Moreover, the person suffering from it requires constant self-care. When it came to my love addiction, I wasn't taking care of myself or admitting to anyone that I suffered from it.

After Julian, my longest relationship lasted nine months with a guy I'll call Lou.

Lou's eyes had a psycho look all the time, like the devil was in them. That should have turned me off, but subconsciously, maybe I was looking for trouble.

I got involved with Lou for the wrong reasons. I pretended to like him when truthfully, I hung out with him because I didn't want to be alone. After only a few dates, I allowed Lou to move into my apartment. Then his abusive and controlling side began to emerge. He didn't allow me to go to meetings, hang with my friends, or do other things that mattered to me. His jealousy led him to break into my Facebook account and delete a platonic male friend from my friend list. He made all kinds of demands, yet he didn't do much. Lou bought food occasionally, but he didn't help with bills.

Plainly put, Lou terrified me and the relationship was mostly sexual. I felt like I had to give him what he wanted in bed to avoid getting hurt. I kept wondering how the hell I was going to escape him.

The longer he stayed in my apartment, the angrier I got, and I couldn't hide it. That made him angry. We started putting our hands on each other. He pushed me. I pushed him. He threw me on my bed to restrain me. I have my father's temper, so I threw shit at him and called him a loser and a waste of life. I told him he wasn't a man.

Then one day, Lou falsely accused me of cheating on him because I wouldn't have sex with him. Then he called me a whore. I spit in his face, pushed him, yelled, screamed, and started throwing his clothes on the floor and telling him to get out of my apartment. He grabbed me, ripped out some of my hair, and threw me down on the floor and then threw me so hard against a wall that I left a big imprint on it. In the midst of all of this, he took my keys and phone so I couldn't leave.

Lou held me hostage for the night, keeping his eye on the front door. In the morning, after we cooled off, I told him he had two days to get out of my place and if he didn't comply, I'd call the cops and have him removed.

The threat worked. Turns out it scared him, for good reason. Later, my friends reported that they had done a background check on him and found out he had felonies and domestic violence charges.

My experience with Lou showed me the great magnitude of my problem with men. I saw that I desperately wanted to be loved no matter the cost to my life, soul, and health. I would get involved with men without even thinking. This knowledge led to a new realization: I needed outside help again, but this time to deal with my relationship problems.

By this point, just several years ago, I was no longer attending as many step meetings as I once had because my business had consumed me; but now I recognized that I had to work a program again because I felt that if I didn't, I might relapse back into drugs.

I began to attend an all-women's group and meet with my sponsor more frequently. But I had also come to realize that the twelve steps and my sponsor could only take me so far, so I started seeing a psychotherapist twice a week too.

Gradually, between the women's group, my sponsor, and my therapist, positive things resulted.

My sponsor suggested that I take some time away from relationships to build a loving relationship with myself. Meanwhile, the women urged me to do the same, and they took it a step further: They advised me to go without sex for a while. Between sessions with the group, my sponsor, and the therapist, I admitted that for most of my life I'd focused on people or things to make me feel better when really I had needed to step back, breathe, relax, sit still, and take care of myself. My sponsor and the others all pointed out that once I *did* take care of myself, all that other good stuff would come together.

With the goal of self-love in mind, I took the suggestion to stay away from relationships and sex to heart. I managed to go without sex for eight months and took myself out on "self-dates" to eat, to the movies, and to travel. I discovered that I enjoyed my own company. I was learning how to be my own best friend.

During this time, my therapist helped me understand why I had been entering into horrific relationships. I had sought out emotionally unavailable men because I always feared that someone would abandon me. The notion of a relationship working out had terrified me because if the guy left, I'd be in the spot Mom occupied after Dad died. Therapy showed me that I might have been suffering more from love avoidance than love addiction.

The therapist helped me understand that healthy people flocked to me but I was the one who did not want to be with them. He showed me that I needed to get over my fear of commitment and be vulnerable to another human loving me in a healthy way.

Therapy also taught me that if I'm constantly finding fault with myself, I will always find fault with others. You know, if I don't feel good enough about myself, why would anyone else be good enough?

During my time of solitude and introspection, I realized that I was grateful to still be here, clean, and getting better. Being alone drowned out the outside noise and let me ponder all of my abusive relationships and begin to correct my course.

My therapist said that my rape at age fourteen stole my ability to say no to sex and bad relationships. In other words, as an adult, I had said yes when many times I had not wanted to do so. But now, I was definitely willing to say no if a situation wasn't right for me.

As I looked in the mirror, I really saw my sadness and understood it. I told myself, *I don't want to live like this anymore. I don't want to keep being with people I don't know and putting myself in harm's way with years clean.*

I came to realize that in a relationship I want emotional intimacy, like having a best friend. I want to talk about anything, to feel safe communicating my feelings. I don't want to have to hide my insecurities and fears. I want to have a partner that I can cry with, snuggle with, watch TV with, dine out with, someone that I can be there for and who can be there for me in the good times and the bad times.

Recently, to my complete surprise, I managed to achieve some of that in a romantic relationship with a woman.

Sky and I knew each other from recovery meetings. We were friends for a few years before anything romantic happened between us.

She pursued me. Sky, a lesbian through and through, took a big risk because I was still uncertain about my sexuality. She wanted to see if we would work out as a couple anyway. Having come through therapy and a timeout from sex, I was willing to give a relationship with Sky a try.

As I write this, I can see her beautiful smile, long black hair, hazel eyes, and skinny frame as we lay in bed watching TV laughing about nonsense, the type of simple things I have longed for in a relationship. We attended concerts and Broadway shows and had deep conversations too.

I enjoyed spending time with Sky, but we experienced conflict. One of our problems stemmed from the fact that we didn't eat together much because she has issues with food. I worried about her eating struggles, but I worried about me more. Sky's body-image problems affected me, like a contagious disease. I started doubting my own looks again, which I hadn't done in years. I'm not heavy any longer—years before, I had succeeded in taking off those thirty-five pounds I'd gained while I dated Julian—but I am not a size 0 like Sky. Fortunately, while she and I dated, I realized that I did not want to be as small as her either.

I liked and trusted Sky. I cared for her more than any woman I have been with, but at the time, I couldn't give her what she needed emotionally, so I attempted to break up with her several times. But Sky didn't want our relationship to end. After several months of this tension, I insisted that we could no longer be together and that the relationship was over.

A few months after our breakup, I ran into her at a meeting. Afterward, we wound up talking for several hours in my SUV and sharing a passionate kiss. After she got back into her own car, I drove away realizing that I had missed her deeply and that I loved her—and that maybe I was *in love* with her. That night, I recognized that I had been resistant to giving our relationship a decent shot because I feared that people might say negative things about me dating a woman. There was no mistaking it—that night, I also realized that, for the first time in my life, I had finally caught real feelings for a woman.

At the time of this writing, I am not dating Sky, but one thing is for sure: My relationship with her answered a longstanding question about my sexual orientation. I believe that I *am* bisexual, something that I had been confused about when I had been with my first girlfriend, Holly. My recent chance encounter with Sky also showed me that to find my romantic happiness, I cannot let what other people think rule my decisions.

In the end, the whole episode revealed to me that it is time for me to feel good about simply being me.

Sky, the all-women's group, and my sponsor and therapist were all godsends. They helped me identify what I want in a romance, which I had not been able to do before. Now, I have hope that I am improving in what is the most painful area of my life: relationships. The fact that I have a better understanding of what will make me happy shows me how much I've grown and how ready I am to finally get this right.

PART FOUR

TRIUMPHING

CHAPTER FOURTEEN

RECOVERY IS NEVER-ENDING

Staying in recovery is a never-ending process. Each day I get out of bed and my feet touch the floor, I make a conscious decision to do the day right. I put on my crystals, feel their healing effects, and connect with my higher power to maintain the best course. For years, these actions have helped me stay clean. Over the years, however, I've discovered that my routine occasionally needs a jolt—a dramatic experience that shows me I have the strength to stay on the right path.

These experiences have included skydiving, hiking, whitewater rafting, cliff jumping, and zip-lining. Of all these things, I love hiking the most.

I've hiked over the past half a dozen years. I started doing it a few years after my relationship with Julian ended, when a friend took me and a bunch of others to upstate New York to climb the challenging Breakneck Ridge mountain. That experience hooked me on hiking.

I love that amazing feeling of accomplishment I experience when I reach a mountain peak, hear silence, and look out at God's amazing work of art. I've hiked in parks and on mountains across the United States. I have a goal to hike in all of the country's parks or as many as I can. I told you I once hated the sound of birds, but now, I love waking up in the morning to nature's music. Hiking is about being outside in the peace that is nature, breathing fresh air, and being grateful to be living in the moment and living clean. Hiking fills me with happiness and a sense of accomplishment. It reminds me of how far I have come.

I can look back and say, *Yes, I climbed that mountain. I am freakin' proud. I'm clean today, and as long as I'm clean and not a slave to my disease of addiction, however it's manifesting itself in the moment, I can accomplish anything.*

With this thought in mind, a few years ago, I took on the most challenging hike of my life: the Grand Canyon.

Some five million people visit the canyon every year, but only about 1 percent of them hike down to the bottom.

I was determined to become part of that elite group, though it would mean no cell phone, no internet, no bathroom, and no showers. It would be nothing but me and a few other people in nature and knowing that the Colorado River, thousands of feet down, and lots of bathing wipes would be my friends.

My tour group consisted of four other people, including a twentysomething-year-old guide, Jackie, thirty-five-year-old Rebecca, Rebecca's fifty-nine-year-old mother-in-law, Anna, and a retired man, Colton, sixty-two. Anna kept us in stitches, occasionally distracting us from the intensity of our hike.

Each of us wore backpacks filled to the brim. I carried forty pounds of gear on my back—folded tent, small foam pad to sleep on, personal hygiene supplies including baby wipes for pee and poop breaks, a garbage bag, water bottles, packaged food like protein bars and trail mix, a few extra T-shirts and other layers, and that's not even half of it. Hiking with that much weight is not easy, not at all!

Before the hike, Jackie had made it crystal clear that after we started our descent, there would be absolutely NO turning back. That put the fear of God in me, but I had flown more than halfway across the country from Long Island and was determined to go through with things. The good news: This would not be a treacherous descent on sharp cliffs but a true downhill climb along broad stretches of the canyon's glorious layers of rock.

But the hike presented many challenges. On our first day, we got stuck in rain and snowfall—*snowfall* in May. But we didn't deviate from our schedule, and in our sweatshirts, gloves, and ponchos we kept walking down that canyon as we froze our asses off. Jackie had given each of us hiking poles to use as we walked in the snow, but I hated them, so I kept mine attached to my backpack. Crazy, huh? Especially because at night we were walking down layers of rock in pitch-dark with only flashlights that were strapped to our heads to provide illumination to guide the way. Between the dark and the cold, I was like, *Please get me to a hotel for the love of God,* but the farther we descended the less and less it rained and snowed and the warmer it became.

As I hiked down that canyon, I thought about what I wanted to do with the rest of my life. In the profoundness of this singular experience, I realized that I wanted to help as many people struggling with addiction as I could. Then the answer of how to accomplish that came to me: by writing a book. I had considered this idea before and had even written down a few words in the past but had gotten nowhere. But now I was done with procrastinating. I thought, *When I get home, I'm writing that damn book!*

After two days, we all made it into the basin of the canyon. When my feet touched the bottom, I smiled, did a little dance around the Colorado River flowing at our feet, and I screamed, "We made it!" My echo boomeranged from canyon walls. I felt giddy, just like a little kid. Then we all scooped up water from the river into our bottles, and Jackie used a portable filtration system to clear out the impurities. Water never tasted so good!

Finally, as I sat in the quiet and peace of the canyon, I felt whole. I can think of no other way to describe it. Being cut off from the world showed me that I could be with myself and other strangers and be myself and silly and that I'm happy and healthy. It also showed me that I could do things on my own and be okay without friends and family no matter how far away I am from them.

After sleeping in the basin, we faced the exhausting climb back up. I made it up the cliffs through a combination of walking and crawling. Thank God we didn't bump into any animals, just one nonvenomous snake that Jackie picked up and threw out of our path. It didn't scare me because she'd told us that it wasn't poisonous.

On day four, close to completing the climb, we finally saw a few other people. They were doing short day hikes. Besides them, we hadn't seen anyone else on our way into the basin and back.

As we neared the top, I was so ready to be done with that damn hike, so I started running toward the "finish line." I was the first one to complete the adventure.

In that moment of accomplishment, I knew that I could do anything that I wanted as long as I had faith in myself and didn't give up.

Another dramatic experience that has helped me stay on the path of self-love and healing was a seven-day retreat in Napa Valley, California. In recent years, I'd been more focused on accommodating clients, speaking at meetings and conventions, sponsoring women in recovery, and showing up for friends. So, I really needed this jolt.

I convened with about forty participants from all over the country. In the confines of a safe space, retreat facilitators encouraged us to be our authentic selves, to say what we needed to say, to yell, scream, cry, hit, laugh, dance, be silly. We felt free to show all the sides of ourselves, sides that usually take years to share with others, so we became emotionally intimate.

The facilitators not only let us be our beautiful selves, they did so much more for me. They dug up every deep thought and feeling I've ever had.

They had a way of helping us heal the broken pieces of our past, starting with childhood, so that we could live in the moment.

We learned that we develop mentally and emotionally in significant ways from birth until age thirteen. During this time, experiences mold us into the people we become. The negativity that we see sticks in our heads more than the positivity. This affects how we view ourselves and others.

Twelve steps and therapy had already shown me that I was wounded inside, that the little girl who had lost her father at age eight was still hurting and that she'd made some bad life decisions because she hadn't understood why. But the retreat helped me take that knowledge deeper. It showed me that I had suffered profoundly because my father was gone. Because Dad had died when I was so young, I had always sought male approval.

I had some positive realizations too, including the fact that I have an awesome family. I recognized that a lot of love filled my house when I was growing up. My father adored me. I was his princess. He would have done anything for me, my brothers, and mother. And though Mom seemed to have trouble expressing emotions when I was younger, she had helped me the best she knew how.

The retreat helped me turn lingering feelings of self-hatred into self-love as well. It taught me that we all have a dark side, that we all have issues that stem from childhood. Everyone has a past. Everyone has addictions, obsessions, and compulsions. I learned that most people find it hard to look in the mirror and love what they see.

Most importantly, I mourned the death of my father for the first time, releasing a waterfall of hot, cleansing tears that racked me to the core of my soul as I finally said goodbye to him. Because I had been a child when he passed, I hadn't known how to mourn. But the retreat helped me understand just how much Dad's death had affected me. The self-knowledge that mourning imbued me with transformed me from a broken little girl into a whole adult person.

The retreat worked a miracle.

CHAPTER FIFTEEN

FAMILY RULES

My story is triumphant not only because I have remained clean and am living to the fullest but because I am now at peace with my family too.

The following journal entry from recent years shows how far I've come.

It's my birthday. I'm thirty-eight years old and have no idea where the time went. My life feels like a dream. Have thirty-eight years really passed? I look in the mirror and see a face that looks more like a twentysomething's. People tell me I look twenty-nineish, which is nice, but the cold, hard reality is that I am way past that.

Sometimes I feel I should have achieved more, but the truth is, I have a good life. No, I don't have the typical life that society or the old school way of thinking says is good. I'm not married with children, and the reality is that I may not have kids. Who knows what the future holds, and although it makes me a little sad to think I won't have children, I also fully embrace where I'm at in life. I hope I will get married one day, but if it doesn't happen, I feel I will still be in a good place. I'm clean, healthy, and have a higher power in my life. I know that whatever is meant to be will be as long as I stay out of my own way, in my lane, and keep doing the right thing for myself.

Today, I'm successful and have the means to do what I want. I can go and come as I please. I hike mountains. I'm a strong, fun-loving woman who just wants to love and be loved and live right.

But I'm a little sad because a big chapter of my life is ending. My mother has sold our family home and is moving to Florida this week. Although our relationship has had many ups and downs, Mom has become my best friend. I used to blame her and everyone else for the bad things that happened to me, but I have learned there is truth in the saying that if you point the finger, you will have three pointing back at you. I now understand that I chose to not ask for help in school. I chose to fail and not wear my glasses and not pay attention. I had a learning disability, but I chose not to study. I chose to cut class, smoke cigarettes, and do drugs. I gave up on myself a long time ago, and I blamed everyone for my choices. Today, because of recovery and staying clean, I see the part I played in the things that happened to me.

I take responsibility for the fact that I chose to never confide in Mom while growing up. I chose to lie to, steal from, and take advantage of her. I have paid her back everything I took from her. I continue to make amends to her every day by showing up for her and myself by becoming a successful, productive member of society and telling her everything. I am honest with her, and this has resulted in dividends for her and for me.

Mom and I have a real mother/daughter relationship now, and this has enriched both of our lives. When I tell her about my relationships, she laughs at my insanity but also tries to get me on the right path, like urging me to avoid certain activities and people and telling me things like, "That guy's not good for you, Marsha." I appreciate that now, and I appreciate what she sacrificed for my brothers and me and her love for us.

I had to recover from active addiction to see how it affected the people who loved me. Like I said at the start of this book, I was a tornado upending everyone's life. That's what makes me appreciate Mom more, because she stuck with me though I inflicted serious pain on her. Okay, yes, for years I was an addict right under her nose and she did nothing about it, but I believe she was in denial. She finally made an effort, however late, to help me. As she tried to pull me up off the cliff of drug addiction, though, I repeatedly yanked my hand away to fall deeper into the cesspool of drugs. I sold many things just to get a few hits of crack or to fill up my syringe with coke or heroin. I sold my guitar and amps. No, I don't play. I learned a bit of guitar, but I gave up on it like I gave up on myself most of my life. But Mom never gave up on me.

Throughout everything, Mom was there. No matter what I stole from her, she stayed in my corner. She was there for me through my breakups, losses of friends and family, starting a business, moving back in, and moving out.

I love her to heaven and back, and I want her to know it.

Being clean has strengthened my relationship with my brothers too.

When I was in my late twenties, the three of us began to reknit our family bonds. This began after my brothers moved from Denver back to New York. We attended weddings, parties, concerts, and Broadway plays together. We wandered around the city and shared beautiful dinners. It was a dream, and we did indeed grow close.

About ten years ago, Eli got engaged, and he and his fiancée asked me to officiate the wedding. They said they loved and respected me a great deal and saw how spiritual I had become. I said yes to their request and received a license from online. Leading their wedding was one of the biggest honors of my life. After they had a child, I had the pleasure of babysitting him. My nephew is brilliant and adorable and calls me "Diddy" because he couldn't say "Auntie" when he was six months old. That name has stuck, so years later, I'm still "Diddy" to him. I love it, and I love that little boy so much.

Rebuilding a relationship with Eli has been wonderful and humbling. We don't see eye to eye on many things, but we are family and we love each other. I love his wife too. They moved to San Diego a few years ago, and I visit as often as possible.

All the visits haven't always been smooth, and that's okay. When I was still making poor relationship choices, Eli admonished me about that time and time again. I always disliked that, but not because I was angry with him. I disliked it because he was always right. He had my best interests at heart and was speaking to me out of love. I am proud to say that I love my family and will forever be grateful to them for standing by me, loving me, yelling at me, and telling me the truth, because that's what you do when you love someone and when you're family—you tell them the truth. Family rules!

As for Noah, he remains nearby, on the Lower East Side of Manhattan. We've built an amazing relationship. He is now one of my best friends. We've traveled across the country and attended many concerts together. I can tell him anything. He doesn't judge me. We hang out and go to Yankees games. When I go away, Noah watches my dog, Joey, a middle-aged Maltese and Yorkie mix, who is very protective of me—no dog can ever replace Heidi, but I love Joey deeply. Noah and I laugh together and cry together. It's just good. He and I are very similar when it comes to relationships. Like me, he's struggled with them. Like me, he's still single.

I had to become a spiritual person to get to this place of loving my family unconditionally. Once I opened my eyes and saw the light, I realized that my mother and brothers are amazing. Every family has a little dysfunction, so I had no reason to be so hard on mine. Now, we all have one another's backs. We love and protect one another. We've seen the other in the darkest of times. Yes, my brothers and I fought and bickered and took advantage of our mom when we were young. We watched her cry over us, take care of us, and almost lose everything after our dad passed. We saw her save the house and save herself. And you know what? She saved us as well. It's hard being a single parent trying to raise three kids. She did the best she could, and we all turned out alright.

Eli is in the education field. Noah is a general manager of a restaurant in New York City. I, of course, own a small business. We all traveled different career paths, but we're all successful.

My family and I beat the odds, and that, my friends, is a blessing. It is a miracle and a gift that I don't take lightly.

CHAPTER SIXTEEN

HEALING OTHERS, HEALING ME

This book wouldn't be complete if I didn't credit my career in massage therapy for playing a major role in my recovery.

Simply put, massage therapy put me on the path to getting clean.

My talent for healing others allowed me to meet people who led me to my own healing. The then-fiancé of my ex-boss at the Fire Island spa first put the notion of the twelve steps in my head, always inviting me to a meeting. My Reiki Master and so many others, from clients to colleagues, urged me to seek treatment. So many people loved me and saw something in me that I couldn't or wouldn't see in myself. Now, I understand that they were placed in my life to lead me to a clean life and spirituality.

I didn't anticipate, however, that traveling on this path would help me grow professionally in ways that would further help me in my recovery. This leads me to Reiki.

As you know, my practice of massage therapy has included Reiki, the laying of hands to bring healing, since almost the start of my career. What you don't know is how and why it has helped me stay clean.

For me, it were as if Reiki was meant to work hand in hand with the twelve steps. The first part of the word, "Rei," means "God's Wisdom" or "Higher Power," a key idea of the spiritually based steps. And like the steps, Reiki, which is spiritually based, has its own set of guiding principles. They emphasize not worrying, not getting angry, working honestly, being grateful for life's blessings, and being kind to people. I learned not only how to apply these principles to my clients but also how to apply them to myself to heal.

Reiki is some strong spiritual medicine. It can heal not only humans you can touch but also plants, animals, a person on TV, and people thousands of miles away that you can't see. It's a form of practicing prayer and meditation through energy.

More than ten years ago, when I began taking master classes in Reiki, I started to undergo a significant change. In each class, my Reiki Master opened my energetic pathways by channeling energy from the universal source, also called a higher power, into me. Afterward, a different form of energy and light surrounded me. As they did, I saw things more clearly. I began to see the world in a brighter, more loving, healing way, which made me more open to the caring people who wanted me to continue to get better and stay clean. I became much more loving toward and understanding of myself and others.

In the past, I had found it much easier to heal other people than to heal myself. But after years of studying to become a Reiki Master, a status I finally achieved about five years ago, I have mastered both.

Today, I work with crystals and aromatherapy and do a lot of energy healing at the spa I bought from Gail. After more than ten years of ownership, it's now a booming holistic healing center, offering comprehensive services to treat people's bodies and spirits. With one touch, I can sense what's going on and my hands know where to travel to heal a client's emotional or physical affliction. I clear their aura and chakras to get rid of negativity to bring in a positive life force. As I tell my clients, that's where the healing lies. Negativity makes us sick, but when we have love and light, true healing can begin.

I have worked on entire families—husbands, wives, children, aunts, uncles. Some of my clients go back to the start of my career twenty-one years ago and have become like family. They encourage me and don't judge me. After I became clean for good, they came back to me. This showed me that they deeply appreciate me and my work; they put their faith and trust in me, and let me tell you, this type of positive energy is one of the things that keeps me in recovery. In return, I work on them with love, which I think they can sense.

These and other clients come to me with a wide range of concerns. I've helped abuse victims learn how to let someone touch them again. I've provided therapy to drug addicts, war veterans, multiple sclerosis sufferers, car accident victims, trauma victims, athletes, children, and people suffering from fibromyalgia, herniated discs, and depression. I have worked on people with cancer for years until the day they died. Before they passed away, a few of them told me they had lived longer partly because of me. I say that's God.

Clients arrive on my table before surgery for the healing effects of massage, which calms their anxiety about going under the knife, and they come back after surgery. I help people who just want to relax too.

People who are in recovery seek my help as well, and while I work to heal them as they lie on my table, they tell me about their alcohol- and drug-use histories. I say, "Hey, me too," and we talk and laugh.

The identification bonds us. When someone in recovery seeks me out, even if I've never met them, right away I know that they've suffered from addiction. I can see it in the glimmer of their eyes, their look of hope. I believe we have a different appreciation for life because we know what it's like to want to die or to be mired in misery. We embrace life a little bit differently than the average person because we were a shell of a human being for so long. But after we get our lives together, we allow ourselves to experience the beauty that surrounds us. We have a different sense of love, joy, freedom, and understanding that we are forever grateful for.

As for me, I am grateful to take my recovery into the outside world as a clean, honest, and hardworking professional. I don't take a moment of that for granted. The woman who was once an active drug addict is now a respected member of society because of her positive actions.

I tell you all this to say that people can and do change; all you have to do is want to change bad enough. Then you need to get out there, seek and accept help, and work for it.

Today, I'm eternally grateful for all the people along the way who showed me how much this thing called life is worth fighting for, because without them, I wouldn't be here. I am thankful for the journey of life, love, and change. I am nothing like who I was in the past, and I love myself wholeheartedly. I am so happy and so fulfilled and grateful for everything I have, everything I don't have, and everything that is coming.

As this book comes to a close, I acknowledge that many of us have suffered from some type of addiction, whether it be drugs, sex, bad relationships, alcohol, food, perfectionism, excessive exercise, cheating, gambling, shopping, workaholism, codependency, and the list goes on. The difference is that most people don't talk about it.

So, here I am saying it out loud: Life is life, and it's going to happen whether we like it or not. Eventually, we will all die, and we never know when our time is going to come. So, if you're struggling with an addiction, today is the day to let it go because we only have so many days on this earth.

Get clean. Live. Have fun. Laugh, dance, cry, scream. Feel. Be your true, authentic self, because we are beautiful just as we are. Don't live someone else's life or someone else's dream.

Don't for a second regret being you.

POSTSCRIPT

Many lessons paved my way through addiction, but for a long time the disease blinded me to them. Fortunately, others cared enough to help me get on the path to recovery and ultimately, find redemption; because of that, today I can reflect on all the lessons that had been right in front of me for years that I could not see.

What follows are some of those lessons. Whether you're in the throes of addiction or in recovery, I hope I can help you see these lessons clearly. Also, I will share anecdotes from my current life that prove that a clean life is worth all the twelve-step work, therapy, introspection, and whatever else you must endure to stay clean.

LESSONS

BEING CLEAN GIVES YOU FREEDOM TO TRAVEL

After I left the Napa Valley retreat, I got on the road, drove along the coast, then checked into a beautiful resort in Calistoga. From there, I traveled to San Francisco, then to Cambria, where I witnessed a magnificent sunset. I drove to Monterey and Big Sur and processed all my feelings. I ended the California trip in San Diego, where I visited my brother Eli, my nephew, and my amazing sister-in-law. Next stop: I flew to Florida to surprise my mother on Mother's Day. This is the freedom I have today: I can do what I want and, sometimes without hesitation, see this beautiful country and my family. Other travel has included Aruba and other Caribbean Islands. I plan to go to more places!

BEING AT PEACE WITH LOVED ONES IS A BENEFIT OF RECOVERY

Recently, I spoke on the phone to my *tante* (Yiddish for "aunt") in the Bronx to make long overdue amends. She's my dad's youngest sister, an old Jewish woman and a Holocaust survivor who doesn't agree with my life choices. She believes that Jewish people should be with Jewish people, so she doesn't understand my choice of romantic partners over the years. She doesn't understand my tattoos; she thinks they're unladylike, to say the least. She doesn't understand my career choice. She definitely doesn't understand my years as an active drug addict. On top of all of that, because I'm not married and don't have kids, her head spins. I just don't fit her idea of what a Jewish woman should be, and over the years she has made that very clear. I stopped talking to her because I thought she didn't like me or accept me; but recovery has shown me that I said some things to make her feel bad too, so she's not the only reason why our relationship suffered.

During our recent conversation, I tried to rebuild a relationship with her as best as I could. Over about an hour, we agreed that a lot of our differences result from the fact that we are from different eras. As we spoke, we attempted to understand each other. Before we hung up, we apologized to each other for the hurtful things we had said in the past. Then I went to sleep happy.

A CLEAN LIFE IS A GOOD LIFE

I'm financially stable and in good shape. I've hiked mountains and in parks across the country. I've spoken at many twelve-step conventions. I've started my own business, made so many friends that will last a lifetime, driven cross-country twice, and been on cruises. I've enjoyed going to the movies, relaxing at home, bowling, shooting pool, and hanging out with friends at barbeques.

I am a lighthearted, fun woman who loves music. I've attended at least 200 rock shows, and I will go to more. Recently, along with my friend Autumn, I met members of Papa Roach, the band whose CD I played repeatedly my first year in recovery. I thanked them for helping me get through the hardest year of my life. Another friend, Connie, also introduced me to one of my favorite bands, 3 Doors Down. I've met a bunch of bands over the years hanging out at shows with Connie, Autumn, and others. I've had so much fun and have had so many amazing experiences and laughed harder than I have ever laughed in my life. If someone had told me years ago I'd have the life I'm living today, I would not have believed it.

Yes, get clean and you are in for some wonderful surprises.

WE ALL DESERVE LOVE

I now believe that someone will come along when God sees fit. I don't want to force any relationships. I just want to really love myself and get mentally healthier. I'm in a good place in my recovery today, so I guess I had to go through it all to get here. I had to do all the drugs, have the sex, date many men, and run around like a muck to realize who I am. It may sound crazy to some people, but I had to go against everything I was to figure out who I truly am.

Once upon a time, I couldn't think of a single good thing about myself. I had absolutely no self-worth or self-esteem. I settled for sex when what I wanted was love. I accepted that because I thought that's all I deserved. My sick thinking told me I wasn't worth more. What a ridiculous mindset!

We all deserve to be loved, to give love, and to be happy. These are not the domains of perfect people. There are no perfect people.

SEX IS EASY, EMOTIONAL INTIMACY IS NOT

In another era, my promiscuous behavior was not the norm—at least not for women. But in this day and age with social media and all these freaking dating apps and whatnot, everyone is so quick to jump into bed. Like whatever happened to dating? They're like, *Want to meet for coffee and if we like each other come back to my house?* In another lifetime, I would have been all into that scene. But today, no way.

I'm now about, *How about let's go to dinner. Can we eat together? Can we talk? Can we hold a conversation? Can we stand each other's company? Do we make each other laugh? Maybe we can see a movie or be dorks and go bowling and be dumb, shoot pool even (though I suck at pool), play video games (although I stink at that too, but it's just fun to do), or play air hockey (I'm actually really good at that).* But no, seriously, what happened to the fun stuff? What happened to getting to know each other, to becoming friends? You're not going to know if you're compatible after one or two dates.

One of the places I messed up with romantic partners: I jumped in the sack with them after having only met their representative. When I say "representative" I mean the good façade we all put on when we meet someone for the first time. The first time, we're all on our best behavior. But after one or two months, people's quirks start to come out.

It's too easy to have sex with the representative. You take your clothes off and don't have to talk. I don't even have to know if you're a good human being, and since I've only met your representative, I surely don't know. Having sex too soon results in an illusion of an emotional connection that probably does not exist.

Today, I need to know what kind of person you are. Now, before I get into bed with you, I want to know how you treat the waitress or the valet or the person who can't do a damn thing for you. Are you nice? Are you prejudiced? Who are you? What do you value? What do you do for a living? What's your favorite color? Here's a good one: What's your last name? Ha-ha. Sad, but true. I've been there. But today, I want to know all this stuff before I jump into bed with you. That can take a month or two to find out.

In other words, sexual intimacy is easy, but emotional intimacy is not.

ADDICTION IS ADDICTION

The biggest lesson that I learned from my drug and love addiction journey is that addiction is addiction. It manifests itself in many ways—drugs, alcohol, sex, shopping, overeating, social media, and on and on. At the end of the day, whatever your addiction vice, it's always about reaching for an outside source to solve an internal problem.

EACH DAY, DECIDE TO DO THE RIGHT THING

Saying I'm sorry is cool, but when you've made a mistake, you've got to do more than apologize. You've got to change your behavior to avoid making the same mistake, committing the same wrong, and hurting someone or yourself again. I've apologized to family members and others for my past transgressions, but I've also changed my behavior to the best of my ability. I strive to be better, not perfect, because perfection is impossible to achieve.

Every day, I make a decision to do the right thing as best as I can. The apology may be necessary, but without changing your behavior that led to the reason for the "sorry," the apology becomes another empty promise. So today, when I say I'm sorry, I mean it. I choose to rectify my behavior a day at a time by proving I'm sorry by not making the same mistake again. I may make new mistakes, but to the best of my ability, I try not to repeat those either. That, my friends, is what we call living in recovery.

NOT ALL MEN ARE MY ENEMY

At one time, I didn't think men were good for anything, but that's because I had a poor attitude about them. Of course, there are good men in the world—plenty. I could not see that because I was always attracting sick people. I was sick as well, and I wasn't always the nicest person. I wasn't always loving and supportive. I gave what I got, and vice versa.

Now that my mind and heart understand that men can be good people too, God has revealed that good men were in my life all along. Among them is my old boss's ex-fiancé (they never got married) who invited me to step meetings when I was in my twenties, with no success. A few years later, I bumped into him at a step meeting, and he was nothing but smiles. He had wanted nothing more from me than that I be okay and live well. I am forever grateful for his example of successful recovery. Though I couldn't see it at the time, he was always my friend.

HAVE HOPE IN LOVE

Recently, one of my best friends in the world, Autumn, got married. I have seen her grow into an amazing woman. I would love to be like her when I grow up. I enjoyed serving as a bridesmaid in her wedding. To share that day with her and her husband was truly an honor, gift, and blessing. My friend and her husband were made for each other. They inspire me. I hope and pray to one day know the kind of love they share. I know it's possible to have. They give me hope in love.

NOT CONFORMING TO SOCIAL NORMS IS OKAY

I've gotten upset with some members of my family and with society because they say your life is supposed to look a certain way—married, kids, house, two-car garage—and if you don't fit the mold, you're some sort of outcast. I've felt like an outcast my entire life because I didn't go with the flow of the "norm," whatever that means. Because of that, I used to get hard on myself instead of loving myself for being a bit weird and different. I used to feel that something was wrong with me for not being married and not having a family of my own. I don't fit the idea of where people think I am supposed to "be" in my life. Maybe the "norm" is not for everyone.

Some people find out I'm single then shoot me a look that says "aww." They feel bad. I'm actually pretty happy most of the time. Yes, I get lonely sometimes, like anyone would. However, I haven't settled for just any person, nor will I. I know plenty of people who have settled because of their age and are miserable because of it. I won't do it. I will be single for a long time if I have to and be happy because nobody is going to complete me except for me.

YOUR PAST DOESN'T DEFINE YOU

Who you were is no longer who you are. The past is the past. To *get* better, we must *be* better.

Everyone makes mistakes. Look at me: I figured out who I am by first figuring out who I wasn't. I put myself through some shit. Who hasn't? We are human and that is life. I love the woman I am because I am who I am because of it all. I have truly forgiven myself and other people and moved on.

I vow to no longer bring the past into my present, and so can you. That, my friends, is what I call FREEDOM.

COMBAT ADDICTION BY CHANGING HOW YOU THINK

Recently, we lost another group member, this time to suicide. This man had thirty years clean. He helped so many people, yet he couldn't help himself. His death shows that the disease of addiction doesn't care how much time we have clean. It is a disease of the mind, so if anyone stands around and talks shit and says this isn't a disease, well in my eyes they can go somewhere, because it *is* a disease and needs constant work and attention.

People can say what they want, but if they don't know what it's like to suffer from the disease of addiction or alcoholism or whatever you want to call it, they don't know what it's like to have the insanity running through their head. I know what it feels like to want to die with years clean, to feel that sense of hopelessness. I've never pulled the trigger because I have constantly chosen to work on myself.

In meetings, we've discussed that a hole exists inside of us that is begging to be filled. We try to fill it with drugs or something else, then we get clean and realize what this disease is really all about. It's about how we think. We are the problem. Our minds are begging to fill our bodies and souls with something else, so now we have to get creative and figure out what other things we can fill them with besides our addiction.

As you know, after active drug addiction, I tried to fill a void in my life with sex, relationships, and work. I made my business my life. I married it. I put it in front of everything, including step meetings, friends, and family. Yes, money ruled. I thought if I had enough money or the right partner, I would feel better. Repeatedly, I tried to fill that hole with outside stuff, including too much food and even overexercising, and nothing worked.

Some say that until you hit rock bottom clean without using drugs, you haven't hit bottom. This is not true for everyone, but it has proven true for me. It's a different type of bottom, not the same as in active addiction, but it's a bottom nevertheless. It doesn't have to end in killing yourself though. We can get help and get better. We can and do. It's about changing how we think. It's about replacing negative self-talk with positive self-talk. It's about seeing ourselves as being worthy of life and all the beauty it has to offer.

Now, my friend chose to die. I don't know what he was thinking. I didn't know the dark side of him. Other people knew it—the mentally ill side, the eating disorder side, the work out until he couldn't work out anymore side. But after I learned about this from others, I understood what he had been trying to do. He had been trying to stop the noise in his head, and I sure do identify with that. At times, I've been right at the edge, screaming inside. But it took my friend killing himself for *me* to see myself in him and to snap out of my own dark thoughts. The expression that goes something like, "Some people have to die for others to live" makes me sad, yet it is true. My friend made me see that I needed to continue on with this thing called life.

TAKE MEDICINE AGAIN WHEN YOU'RE READY

For a long time after getting clean, I refused to take antidepressants. As you know, I wanted to take control of my mental state on my own, not through medication. I did not want to become dependent on pills. But a few years ago, I took a leap of faith and accepted my doctor's recommendation to take an antidepressant for episodes of constant crying and despair. I had to be clean for thirteen years before I could trust myself to do this. Fortunately, I discovered that I did not become dependent on the drug; I believe this is because of the grace of God and years of getting strong in my recovery. Take your own leap of faith only when you feel the time is right. Only you will know when that time has come.

SETTING BOUNDARIES IS CRUCIAL

Certain things are off-limits, like romantic partners in active addiction. I now know I can't save these people; they have to save themselves. I'm not going to be the person they fall in love with, that they're going to want to be a better person for. That's a fantasy.

Time and time again, I put myself through the ringer thinking I could change someone, yet I had a hard time changing my own codependent self. Now, I understand that it's better to love and honor myself than to try to find love and honor in someone who is not clean, or someone who is married or in a relationship, or someone who does not have a job, a place to live. You know, basic stuff! All of these people are off-limits. I have to set these kinds of boundaries to stay in recovery.

SELF-LOVE AND SELF-CARE ARE IMPORTANT

For many years, I wanted attention, negative or otherwise. Negative attention was better than nothing. That desire continued into my recovery. Now, I've become committed to stopping this cycle of insanity. How do I do that, each and every day? By taking care of myself. This is called self-love and self-care.

What is self-love and self-care? It is eating right. It is working out within reason. It is taking care of my spirit by filling it with God, prayer, and meditation. I light candles to breathe in aromatherapy. I get manicures, pedicures, massages, facials, and body scrubs. I go to step meetings, to dinner, concerts, hang with friends, shoot pool, listen to music, hang with my dog, travel. I have stopped saying yes when I mean no. No more people pleasing for me. If I don't want to go out to a party or gathering, I stay home. If I am overworked, I say, "No, I can't do it tonight." If I don't want to have sex, I say, "No."

Someone once told me that NO is a full sentence and that I don't have to explain myself to anyone. Now, I stay true to myself and my belief systems. I live my morals, my values, and my truth. This practice is all about self-love and self-care.

LISTEN AND FOLLOW DIRECTIONS

I'm in a great place today because, for the most part, I'm finally listening to, and following, directions. Twelve-step literature says we have a hard time making consistently good decisions for ourselves, and that has proven true for me. I need to follow directions because left to my own devices, I will make harmful choices. The longer I stay clean, the more I realize how real that is, and the better I get, the more I can see the sickness in other people. Don't get me wrong. I've made amazing decisions in business and other areas; but as you know, I have fallen short in relationships. So, I listen to my sponsor when she advises me about my romantic partners. To save myself from detrimental impulses, I know that I must listen to, and follow, directions.

RECOVERY HELPS YOU DEAL WITH BREAKUPS LIKE AN ADULT

I don't chase people today. If someone says they don't want to be with me, I allow them to walk out the door gracefully. I can cry about it. I can call my friends. Maybe I will go to a meeting and cry because that's what I have been taught to do. We stay clean by talking things out and crying. But I do not beg or chase people, and I certainly don't make an ass out of myself. Acting crazy doesn't do anyone any good. When a relationship is over, it's over. I don't have to like it all the time. I accept it though and act like a person in recovery.

RECOVERY HELPS YOU ACCEPT WHO YOU ARE

I wasted a lot of time suffering from low self-esteem, but as I got older, I began to understand that accepting and loving myself just the way I am, the beautiful person that God made me to be, is the key to personal freedom.

How do you accept yourself? I made myself feel better about who I am by being better, by acting better, by living my truth and not compromising my personal morals and values. I started by asking myself who I wanted to be. Ask yourself: *Who do I want to be? What kind of mother, daughter, sister, brother, father, boss, worker, coworker, significant other do I want to be? What are my goals? How do I want to live?* Focus on the good, because focusing on the negative gives life to the darkness. When you focus on the positive, however, you give love and light to the universe and your self-acceptance blossoms.

WHEN YOU FALL, GET BACK UP

A long time ago, I learned that I better stand for something or I'll fall for anything. The lesson goes back to my childhood when my parents taught me how to ride a bike. When I fell off it, they encouraged me to get back on and keep riding. By example, they taught me that when life throws you down, you have to get back up to have a shot at success. Years later, after relapsing, I kept getting back up to try to get clean again, and finally, on February 2, 2004, I achieved success. Over the years, I have fallen down in other areas of my life, but like my parents taught me, I get back up, and I come back stronger—not perfect, but better.

DON'T LET FEAR HOLD YOU BACK

For a long time, my fears and false belief systems held me back from success. Only after I told my negative thoughts to shut up did my life start to change. I had to fail a thousand times before I could succeed and win. Everyone's success looks different because everyone wants different things. Just know that whatever you want to do, go for it. Try and then try again.

The only things I have ever regretted are the things I haven't had the courage to face and things I wanted to, but didn't, try. I feared writing this book. I feared getting clean. I feared starting my own business. I feared going on meds to heal from hepatitis C. I feared making amends to my family. I feared the steps. I feared losing weight and changing my lifestyle. I feared gaining weight. I feared change because who would I be without all this stuff I had kept locked and loaded in my head for so long? I feared letting go of my defects that I felt protected me. I feared it all, but I didn't let my fear control me because I busted through my fear and did it all.

I feared traveling alone, cliff jumping, going to concerts alone, and jumping out of a plane. I feared entering into a new relationship, because what if my heart got broken again and the relationship became unhealthy. Now, I don't fear that. And I don't fear the other things I mentioned because I did them all. I conquered them because I didn't want to stay trapped in my fears.

MY HIGHER POWER WATCHES OUT FOR ME

I know God—my higher power, the universe—has my back. Without fail, my higher power has done for me what I can't do for myself. Knowing this keeps me sane and moving in the right direction.

BE GRATEFUL FOR YOUR SCARS

I am grateful for the scars on my arms from the needles I used for years. They remind me of where I come from and where I never want to go back to.

HAPPINESS IS AN INSIDE JOB

I've learned that no person, place, or thing can make me happy. Happiness is an inside job, and until you really love yourself, you won't know how to truly love anyone else. Fortunately, today I can honestly say that I love myself, that I am happy.

CHOOSE TO FEEL

Giving up drugs means I choose to feel, because prior to getting clean, drugs numbed me.

So clean, I choose joy and happiness. I choose sadness and to cry. I choose to deal with life, the death of loved ones, buying a business, buying a car. I choose to be a responsible adult. Because I choose to feel, I have become aware of what I really want. I have learned a new, better way to live because I choose to feel.

EVERY ACTION DOES *NOT* DESERVE A REACTION

I used to always need to say something or do something to get my point across. Sometimes, I fought physically or argued over the silliest things or because someone's opinion differed from my own. Today, I have learned that most of the time it's better to walk away from a disagreement, especially when the other person is close-minded and would never be swayed. This has lessened my stress and helped me reserve my energy for worthier battles. This is the priceless gift of knowing that not every action deserves a reaction.

IF YOU'RE STRUGGLING, YELL

Sometimes, we feel there is no way out of our thinking. Sometimes, we feel hopeless, like there is no way out but death. But I am here to say that there is always a way out—a better way. We don't have to die. So, if you're struggling, yell about it, scream about it. Whatever you do, hang on and fight for your life! There is always a way to get better. There is always hope in even our most desperate hour. Even when our hearts are breaking and we feel so desperate that we want to die, we don't have to harm ourselves.

When I felt the urge to do self-harm, I did what I was taught to do—I talked, yelled, screamed, cried, and shared my thoughts even when I sounded like a complete lunatic. Trust me, plenty of times I sounded like I was completely out of my mind, and I'm not gonna lie—yeah, I cared what other people thought. But I had to say things out loud to others to save my life because I didn't want to die.

Every day, I choose to fight for my life because I know I am worth it. If that means going to a meeting to cry, that's what I'm going to do. My life is worth the battle. Just remember, life is beautiful and full of endless positive possibilities.

Tomorrow can always be a better day if you give it a chance.

SELF-ACCEPTANCE IS AN ONGOING PROCESS

Although I accept myself now more than ever, sometimes I still suffer from low self-esteem and lack of self-acceptance. The bad feelings are not nearly as bad as they were, but they are there.

My various addictions stemmed, in part, from lack of self-love and self-acceptance and not wanting to feel anything, whether it be love or loss. But I'm learning how to deal with my feelings in a healthy way. I'm allowing myself to cry and to feel pain without running to a guy or drugs or a box of cookies to fix things.

Now, I understand that it's okay when my feelings get hurt, that I don't need to act out because of it. Instead of chasing after someone else, I'm filling myself with God and self-love. I'm finally starting to accept myself and life circumstances on a deeper level. This doesn't mean I don't feel the pain. It doesn't mean that I'm not uncomfortable. I *am* uncomfortable, and I *am* still in pain. I can, however, get through it without acting on my feelings.

My sponsor tells me it's okay to love myself, that it's not conceited to own and know my worth and to see myself as awesome and beautiful. She tells me to remember that I am a respected woman because I've become respectable. She says, "Once you truly embrace who you are as a woman, you will no longer accept the unacceptable again."

She is right, and I can wholeheartedly say that I am finally there. I always hold myself in a confident manner in a room full of people because I *am* confident. I walk in with my head held high and speak with assuredness. I'm loud and funny. I can see myself the way other people see me—as an amazing, confident, beautiful, successful, intelligent, and free-spirited woman with the whole entire world ahead of me.

CHOOSE TO BE POSITIVE

I'm grateful for what I have and the life I've gained because I have worked damn hard to get here. I am a self-made success story, and I am proud of that. I could choose to focus on all the bad decisions I've made, but I choose to focus on where I am today and the good decisions I make.

Now, I can truly appreciate the change of seasons, food, business, success, traveling, and adventures. There is so much good, beauty, and joy in this world. That's what I choose to focus on. That's right: Being positive is a choice.

STEER YOUR OWN BOAT

When I was using drugs, I didn't have consequential thinking. I wanted what I wanted when I wanted it. I was impulsive. As a result, I handed myself a lot of unnecessary pain. All I had to do was listen and heed sound advice, but I didn't. I was rebellious. I thought I knew everything, but I knew nothing. I certainly didn't know what was best for me. Those who were clean or had never used a drug a day in their lives advised me to get my act together and urged me to go into rehab. I thought these people were telling me what to do, and yes they were; however, their prodding was coming from a place of love and experience.

They told me I shouldn't use drugs because continuing to do so would continue to cause me pain. But with my stubborn and rebellious nature, I did whatever I wanted to do, and in return, I paid a hefty mental and physical price. My friends and family tried steering me in a better direction, but until I was willing to listen to them, I could never get on the right course. When I finally did listen and start improving myself, I realized it was up to me to chart my own way. My friends and family could advise and even help me get on the boat, but they couldn't steer it for me. I had to take the wheel. Now, I am definitely doing that. And what do you know? My life is so much more peaceful and calm. There is no chaos. There are no catastrophes. I live at peace and in happiness because I have learned the art of life navigation.

BE GRATEFUL FOR WHO YOU ARE

If Dad had lived, I would not have been a drug addict or promiscuous. Honest to God, I think I would have gone to a four-year college, married a Jewish guy, and had kids. I don't know what career path I would have taken, but it would not have been massage therapy. And I would not have been an independent woman.

I wouldn't be as smart as I am today. A sheltered upbringing would have made me more fearful of life. Limited experiences would have robbed me of the ability to see through people. I would not be as empathic.

I miss Dad every day, but I don't dwell on that or feelings of "what if." I am grateful for my life now and who I have become. I am grateful to be a massage therapist and Reiki Master. I am grateful for the opportunity to heal others.

THIS ONE IS FOR YOU, PARENTS

For the parents out there, pay close attention to your children because you never know what is going on in their heads and their lives. Have that uncomfortable conversation about sex and drugs with them. Listen and watch their attitudes and behaviors. Take notice of who they're keeping company with, and if you, for a second, feel something is wrong, your gut is probably right. If, for a second, you think your kid is on drugs, then have them tested for drugs because you may be able to save their life by forcing them to get honest. Stand outside the bathroom as they pee in the cup. Check them beforehand to make sure that they don't have someone else's sample on them!

Paying close attention can be hard for all parents, especially single parents who have so much on their plates. But make the time to do this. It is critical for the health of your child and the health of your family. It is critical for your health too.

Some think living in denial is easier than facing reality. Your child may be crying out for help and want and need you. Show that you care enough about them by leaving your job, boyfriend or girlfriend, or event so that you can pick your kid up from that party. Do this so they don't get in the car with someone who is drinking or doing drugs.

Talk to your children so that they can feel safe enough to call you when they need you. Put fear into them about the dangers of substance abuse. Tell them the horror stories about young people who have died from drinking or using drugs. Show that you are open to listening to them. Do this so that they can feel they can trust you enough to call you when they are at a party that is getting out of hand. Don't misunderstand me. I'm not saying be their best friend. I'm saying talk to them and pay attention so that they feel comfortable enough to be honest with you.

ACKNOWLEDGMENTS

I truly don't know where I would be without you, Brett. You are the person who encouraged me to write this book. I love you and your family. I want to thank you for being my friend and for always being honest with me, having faith in me, encouraging me, never judging me, and for all the good times and for all the laughter. I am forever grateful for our friendship.

To Ezra, you have never once let me down and never steered me in the wrong direction. You encouraged me to keep going with this book even though I was scared to put myself and my truth out there. All your positive and encouraging words helped me continue on this path. You've been there for me as a cheerleader, advisor, and a friend who loves me without judgment. I am eternally grateful for you.

Mom, we've had many ups and downs, but our relationship is stronger than ever. Thank you for guiding me to become an independent, strong woman. I can stand on my own feet because you taught me how to do so. Thank you for being there for me and not giving up on me even when I gave up on myself. I love you with all that I have. I will forever continue on this path of recovery and self-discovery to grow a day at a time into the God-centered woman that I am supposed to be. I will keep on making you proud.

Eli and my sister-in-law, thank you both for blessing this family with the biggest and best gift, my nephew. He has been the light this family needed to bring us back together to remember all the good stuff and all the love. Thank you, sister-in-law, for all those great, deep talks and for allowing me to open up to you and cry. Thank you for loving me where I am. Thank you, brother, for always telling me the truth even when I don't want to hear it. No matter what our differences have been, you have always stood by my side. I love you so much.

Noah, my brother, I love you dearly. We will probably end up like the brother and sister from *Eight Crazy Nights* (Ha, inside joke!). You never once judged me and my relationships and have always been there for me, like a best friend. You are my biggest cheerleader and have always been so proud of the person I have become. You show up at my anniversaries and give me my recovery coin most years. You mean the world to me. Thank you for always standing in my corner.

Dad, I promise I will stay on this path of recovery and keep making you proud. You have been the angel looking over my shoulder all these years. Your spirit gave me the courage and strength to get back up and keep fighting and not give up on myself. Over the years, you've given me many signs. The one thing I always wanted was for you to be proud of the woman I would become. Today, I can say with great certainty that I am that woman. I feel you beaming with pride.

My sponsors, thank you all for putting up with me and loving me until I could learn to love myself. Thank you for guiding me in this process and for never judging me. You always had my best interests in mind. I'm grateful that I can trust you all and talk to you about anything and everything. Thank you, thank you, thank you.

Everyone I have sponsored over the years, thank you for trusting me with your step work and the stories of your lives. It's been an honor and a privilege to watch you grow and mature into the amazing women that you are today. You all—we all—are truly miracles. You have helped me stay clean a day at time. We do this, and we do it together. I love you all. Thank you.

My editor and coauthor, Cheryl Ross, you are absolutely amazing and a godsend. You have the patience of a saint and have worked very hard to make this into a book. If not for you, this book wouldn't be possible. You guided me without judgment. I thank you for making me feel comfortable and safe enough to share my written recollections with you and to open up in all the interviews. I know in my heart of hearts that I put this labor of love in the right hands. Words can't express my appreciation. I am so grateful for you.

My best friend and sister, Autumn, and your awesome husband, I thank you both for showing me what true love and friendship are about. I thank you both for all your love, support, and encouragement. You mean the world to me.

I thank every man who has come into my life romantically. You all taught me valuable lessons. All of my experiences with you led me to the path of self-discovery, and although the breakups devastated me, I came away from them understanding myself that much more.

All my friends in recovery—I can't possibly point all of you out—we've been by one another's side watching our struggles, successes, loves, and losses. We got ourselves out of the trenches, and we learned a new way to live. We don't use anymore! We got to this point together. I love you all.